1994

S0-AGQ-843

# BILLIE HOLIDAY

*Bud Kliment*

MELROSE SQUARE PUBLISHING COMPANY
LOS ANGELES, CALIFORNIA

Senior Consulting Editor for Chelsea House
Nathan Irvin Huggins
Director
W.E.B. Du Bois Institute for Afro-American Research
Harvard University

Consulting Editor for Melrose Square
Raymond Friday Locke

Originally published by Chelsea House, New York, New
Haven, Philadelphia. © 1990 by Chelsea House.

Cover Painting: Jesse S. Santos
Cover Design: Jeff Renfro

# BILLIE HOLIDAY

# MELROSE SQUARE BLACK AMERICAN SERIES

ELLA FITZGERALD
*singer*

NAT TURNER
*slave revolt leader*

PAUL ROBESON
*singer and actor*

JACKIE ROBINSON
*baseball great*

LOUIS ARMSTRONG
*musician*

SCOTT JOPLIN
*composer*

MATTHEW HENSON
*explorer*

MALCOLM X
*militant black leader*

CHESTER HIMES
*author*

SOJOURNER TRUTH
*antislavery activist*

# CONTENTS

# Chapter One

# A Crucial Engagement

AS THE HOUR approached midnight on March 27, 1948, thousands of music lovers converged on 57th Street in New York and filed into Carnegie Hall, one of the city's most prestigious concert halls. The men and women who made up this large group of ticket holders came from all walks of life. "Platinum mink rubbed shoulders with worn tweed," noted one observer. "Music critics smiled at young, poorly clad kids, Harlem sat next to Park Avenue."

The audience had come to hear an Easter eve concert that had first been announced two weeks earlier in the *New York Daily News*. A

*Holiday takes the stage at New York's Carnegie Hall on March 27, 1948. She called this return to performing, which occurred just 10 days after she finished serving a federal-prison sentence for possession of narcotics, "the biggest thing that ever happened to me."*

small notice in the paper had served as the show's lone advertisement. It read: "One night stand. Carnegie Hall. Billie Holiday. March 27." Yet that tiny message, which ran just eight times, had been enough to cause the show to sell out.

Many people considered the 32-year-old Holiday to be the world's most distinctive jazz vocalist. For almost 17 years, she had performed regularly in New York City, garnering a large following wherever her bittersweet voice filled the air: in Harlem night spots, Greenwich Village cafés, and clubs on the midtown block known as Swing Street. But then she left the music scene. By March 1948, when her late-night show at Carnegie Hall was announced, she had been absent from the stage for almost a year. Accordingly, her fans thrilled at the prospect of hearing her perform again in New York City. Lady Day, as they called her, was coming home at last.

By the night of the concert, anticipation over Holiday's return had swelled to an electrifying pitch. Because the demand for tickets to her comeback engagement was so overwhelming, extra chairs were placed onstage so that 300 additional fans could attend the show. Nevertheless, this added measure failed to accommodate thousands more of her admirers who came to the theater's box office only to be turned away, disappointed.

Holiday was among those who understood that the show had become more than a jazz concert—it had turned into an event. Seated in her backstage dressing room before the

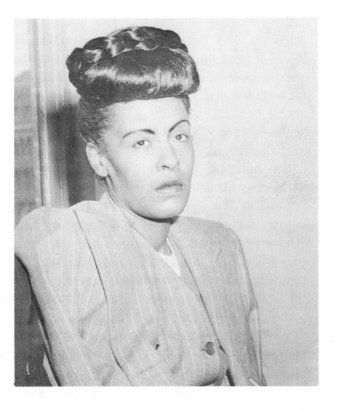

*Holiday in May 1947, at the time of her arrest on a narcotics charge. The case, she said, "was called the United States of America versus Billie Holiday. And that's just the way it felt."*

start of the concert, she sensed the air of expectation that surrounded her return. She was aware, too, of the irony of the situation. There she sat, preparing to sing to a capacity crowd at one of the leading concert halls in the world, when only 11 days earlier she had been a lonely inmate in prison.

Holiday had not performed in public for almost a year because she had been serving time for possession of narcotics. In 1941, she had begun using heroin, and she had quickly become hooked on the drug. By the mid-1940s, she had become a full-fledged addict with a habit that required her to spend $500 a week on the narcotic. (An equivalent habit today would cost almost four times as much.)

Then, in the spring of 1947, Holiday got caught. Agents of the U.S. Bureau of Narcotics arrested her and charged her with drug possession. She stood trial on May 27, and the presiding judge sentenced her to serve a year and a day at the Federal Reformatory for Women at Alderson, West Virginia.

To Holiday, who had grown accustomed to expensive gowns, lively nights, and loud applause, Alderson seemed to belong to another world. The reformatory was a desolate place consisting of 6 small houses, with 50 to 60 women quartered in each building. Nearly half the prisoners were black, and they were forced to eat, sleep, and worship separately from the white inmates because Alderson, like virtually all Southern institutions in the late 1940s, was racially segregated.

Even though Holiday had experienced great hardship on account of racial inequality many times before, Alderson's policy of segregation was not easy to bear. Moreover, it was not the only difficulty she had to face in prison. She also had to go through drug withdrawal because the authorities would not allow her to use the narcotics to which she had become addicted.

Forced to end her heroin addiction cold turkey, Holiday spent the first month of her sentence in quarantine. For 19 days, her body seemed to revolt against itself as she attempted a complete and abrupt withdrawal from the drug. She shook violently, suffered chills, and barely slept or ate. "The first nights I was ready to quit," she said of the experience. "I thought I'd just explode."

Nevertheless, Holiday managed to make it through the agonizing withdrawal period. She then settled into the dull routine of prison life. Initially, she was assigned to work on the prison farm, picking vegetables and taking care of the pigs. Yet her body was still ravaged from her years of drug addiction, and she was unaccustomed to strenuous labor. On one excruciatingly hot day, she collapsed from sunstroke.

Deciding that Holiday was not at all suited to work outdoors, the prison authorities ordered her to cook and clean in one of the prison houses. She prepared the meals and did the dishes, washed the windows and scrubbed the floors, and brought buckets of coal up from the cellar. Apart from carrying the coal, which was used to keep the stove lit and the house heated, she did not mind her new duties very much.

The sense of isolation that accompanied prison life was an entirely different matter. Alderson cut Holiday off from her friends and fans, from everyone she knew and loved. Being alone wore heavily on her, and prison regulations did not make the situation any easier.

The rules at Alderson dictated that inmates could receive only letters sent by their immediate families. Because both of Holiday's parents were dead and she knew of no other living relatives, she was not permitted to read any of her mail, even though her friends and thousands of her fans from around the world had written to her, offering their support and love. The warden, sympathetic to Holiday's situation, eventually intervened on her behalf and allowed her to receive three letters a week.

But Holiday's mood barely improved. Many of the inmates, aware of her talent and reputation, asked her to sing for them, but she refused. The warden requested that she take part in the amateur talent shows held regularly by the prisoners. Holiday said no. Lonely, separated from the world, she argued that she had nothing to sing about. "The whole basis of my singing is feeling," she said later. "In the whole time I was there I didn't feel a thing."

*Following her conviction on drug charges in May 1947, Holiday was sentenced to serve a year and a day at the Federal Reformatory for Women at Alderson, West Virginia. "I didn't think there was anyone who would help me," she said. "And worse, I had been convinced that nobody* could *help me."*

But Holiday somehow persevered, making up her mind to stay in line and perhaps win an early release for good behavior. After 8 months of being a model inmate, she was told that the prison review board had decided to reduce her sentence by 72 days. When March 16, 1948, arrived, she would be released on parole.

Upon hearing this good news, Holiday's manager, Joe Glaser, immediately booked her to play Carnegie Hall. He scheduled her return to the professional ranks for March 27—an arrangement that left her only 11 days to prepare for the show. Bobby Tucker, a pianist who was a close friend of Holiday's, offered to help her get ready.

As soon as Holiday was released from Alderson, she took a northbound train and met Tucker at the station in Newark, New Jersey. They got in his car and drove to his mother's house in nearby Morristown, hoping that Holiday would be able to rehearse undisturbed and unwind more easily if she was away from the New York limelight. When they entered the house, Holiday's eyes filled with tears. She saw that Tucker's family had kept its Christmas tree lit for her even though it was well past the holiday season.

The scene at Holiday's first rehearsal was nearly as emotional. As they got under way, she told Tucker that she had not sung in prison and was not sure how well her voice would sound. All the same, she asked him to play "Night and Day," a popular Cole Porter tune that had always given her trouble. Tucker played the opening chords slowly, then Holiday joined in. "I'll never forget that first note, or the second," she said later. "Or especially the third one, when I had to hit 'day' and hold it. I hit it and held it and it sounded better than ever. Bobby almost fell off the stool, he was so happy. And his mother came running out...and took me in her arms."

Holiday replayed this happy scene in her head as she sat backstage at Carnegie Hall a week later. If only starting over could be that simple. A year was a long time to be away from the stage, and she had not exactly been on vacation. Moreover, many people disapproved of ex-convicts and drug addicts, whether they had reformed or not. One radio station even went so far as to ban her records from the airwaves.

Even though Holiday knew her voice was as powerful as ever, she remained filled with doubt. Had the concert sold out because the public really wanted to hear her sing, or was the house full simply because she had become a curiosity? This engagement would provide the answer. She got up from her seat and walked tentatively to the wings of the stage, where she waited with Bobby Tucker and three other backup musicians as the house-lights dimmed and the audience grew quiet. Reflexively, she smoothed down the sides of

her dress.

Fred Robbins, a New York disc jockey, stepped onto the stage and strode to the microphone to introduce Holiday. A deafening roar went up from the crowd as she walked slowly into the spotlight. According to the jazz periodical *Down Beat*, it was "one of the most thunderous ovations ever given a performer in this or any other concert hall." Holiday waited for the cheering to die down, then launched into her first number, "I Cover the Waterfront." By the time the song was over, it had become clear to the entire audience that the singer's stay in prison had not affected her ability to perform.

The set continued with Holiday tackling several of her most popular songs with consummate ease. At the end of each tune, the audience's response seemed to grow louder. *Time* magazine later reported that the "hysterical applause gave the event the quality of a revival meeting."

There was a brief intermission after 15 songs. Backstage, Holiday said that she felt

---

*According to Frank Sinatra, "Billie Holiday was, and still remains, the greatest single musical influence on me. I think anyone listening to Billie sing can't help but learn something from her."*

"elated." She changed into a black dress, then spotted some gardenias that a fan had sent her. Touched that "somebody had remembered" that the flowers were her trademark, she placed them in her hair without realizing that a hat pin lay hidden beneath the blossoms. Her head began to bleed because of the sharp pin. Bobby Tucker took one look at her and grew alarmed. "Lady, you can't go on," he said. "You must be dying." But Lady Day, bent on finishing this crucial performance, washed off the blood and returned to the stage, hiding her discomfort from the crowd.

Holiday began the second set with "Don't Explain." More tunes followed, including "All of Me," "My Man," and "Solitude." As the set drew to a close, she began to feel weak. She motioned to Tucker to skip "Night and Day" and move on to the last song, "Strange Fruit," which had become her signature number. When she finished, the crowd was on its feet, asking for more. Now that Lady Day had finally come home, they did not want to let her go. She took two curtain calls before collapsing backstage.

Holiday's midnight show at Carnegie Hall—described by Tucker as "the musical treat of my life"—lasted more than two and a half hours. It was one of the milestones of her career. She had never performed more brilliantly, nor to a more appreciative audience. But, as was so often the case for her, good fortune did not hold out. In the years that followed her Easter concert, she met repeatedly with trouble, both privately and professionally, at times creating the difficulties herself.

As though following some erratic inner rhythm, Billie Holiday's life constantly alternated between triumph and tragedy. Hardship was always mixed in with success—even from the beginning.

## BILLIE IN STRONG N.Y. COMEBACK; 7G GATE

Billie Holiday's comeback concert at Carnegie Hall, Saturday (27), indicates that her confinement at a federal hospital for nearly a year hasn't dimmed her popularity or skill. On what is traditionally considered one of the worst nights in show business, the eve before Easter Sunday, Miss Holiday drew a packed hall, with 300 standees, who paid a record gate of $7,100, of which Miss Holiday got a $2,500 cut.

*In its review of Holiday's return engagement at Carnegie Hall, the entertainment newspaper* Variety *said, "A year hasn't dimmed her popularity or skill."*

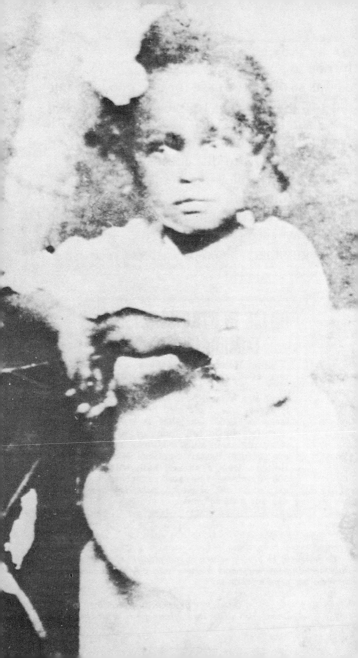

# Chapter Two

# Young and Tough

BILLIE HOLIDAY WAS born Eleanora Fagan on April 7, 1915, in Baltimore, Maryland. Her parents, Sadie Fagan and Clarence Holiday, were not married at the time of her birth. As Holiday put it in her autobiography, *Lady Sings the Blues*, her parents were "just a couple of kids"—in love but unprepared. In fact, when they did marry, Clarence attended the wedding in his very first pair of long pants.

Shortly after their marriage, the newlyweds moved with their daughter to a four-dollar-a-week residence on Durham Street in East

*Holiday at the age of three. She grew up in Baltimore, Maryland, where she endured an extremely difficult childhood.*

Baltimore. There, it seems, they were happy for a time. While Eleanora's father took trumpet lessons with the hope that he would someday become a professional musician, her mother worked as a maid. Eventually, they managed to save enough money to have gas and electricity installed in their house—the first in the neighborhood to have such conveniences.

But World War I interrupted the family's plans. When the United States entered the war in 1917, Clarence was drafted and sent to Europe to fight in the trenches. There he inhaled poison gas employed by the German army. The resulting damage to his lungs ended his dream of playing the trumpet for a living. But all was not lost. While recovering in Paris, Clarence learned to play the guitar. By the time he returned home to Baltimore, he had mastered the instrument, and he soon began playing professionally, touring the country with jazz bands led by such prominent musicians as Don Redman and Fletcher Henderson.

Clarence's success had a downside, though. The traveling took him away from his wife and child. His daughter later said of her father that "when he went on the road...it was the beginning of the end of our life as a family. Baltimore got to be just another one-night stand." Eventually, Sadie Holiday filed for divorce.

The absence of her husband forced Sadie to provide single-handedly for herself and her daughter. After working for a while at a factory, she again found employment as a maid, one of the few jobs then available to black women. People in Baltimore paid their maids poorly, however, so Sadie decided to head north, where she could earn more money working for wealthy families in Philadelphia

*Holiday hailed from a musical family. Her father, Clarence (back row, far right), played guitar in one of the nation's first jazz bands, which was directed by Fletcher Henderson (front row, third from right).*

and New York. Like her former husband, Sadie had to take to the road to earn a living.

With her mother away from Baltimore most of the time, Eleanora stayed with her cousin Ida. Sadie returned to Baltimore to see her daughter whenever the opportunity arose. But for Eleanora, the visits were never long enough. She hated living in her cousin's tiny house. In addition to Ida and her two children (with whom Eleanora had to share a bed), her maternal grandparents and great-grandmother also resided there. The cramped conditions wore on Ida, and she often took it out on Eleanora, not only by yelling at her but also by beating her.

Eleanora found a reprieve from Ida's abuse in her friendship with her elderly great-grandmother. "She really loved me and I was crazy about her," Holiday recalled. "We used to talk about life." Eleanora's great-grandmother had been a slave, and she would converse with the young girl for hours about plantation life and how it felt to be owned "body and soul by a white man." She also spoke of Charles Fagan, the white plantation owner who had been her master and the father of her 16 children. Those stories marked Eleanora's first exposure to black history, and they remained with her for the rest of her life.

Sadly, Eleanora's love for her great-grandmother led to one of the most traumatic experiences of her youth. The old woman suffered from a disease called dropsy (also known as edema), which made it dangerous for her to lie down because an abnormal amount of fluid might accumulate in her abdomen. Night after night, for more than 10 years, she had had to sleep sitting upright in a chair. One day, feeling exhausted, she begged Eleanora to let her rest on the floor. Not knowing any better, the child agreed. Eleanora smoothed a blanket over the hard surface, and the two of them lay down side by side. The old woman put her arm around the child and began to tell her a story from the Bible. Eleanora soon drifted off to sleep.

When she awoke several hours later, Eleanora saw that her great-grandmother had stopped breathing. Eleanora tried to get up, but the old woman's bony arm had stiffened around the young girl's neck and would not loosen. Terrified, Eleanora began to scream. Some neighbors finally heard her cries and came into the house to assist her. They had to break the dead woman's arm to free Eleanora.

Devastated by the loss of her great-grandmother, Eleanora had to be confined to a hospital for a month to calm her troubled nerves. Upon recovering, she returned to her cousin Ida's—and received more beatings. A doctor from the hospital tried to stop the abuse but was not successful. "So Ida started right in where she had left off," Holiday recalled.

Having to go to school helped get Eleanora out of the house. She managed to make it through the fifth grade, although she often cut classes to sneak into Baltimore's Royal Theater and watch movies. Her favorite film star was Billie Dove, and she began calling herself Billie instead of Eleanora, boasting that she wanted to be just like the actress when she grew up.

Eleanora's adopted name was a hint of glamour in an otherwise bleak existence. She spent most of her youth in terrible poverty, her childhood cut short by the need to earn money. "I never had a chance to play with dolls like other kids," Billie said. "I started working when I was six years old."

Before and after school, Billie baby-sat or scrubbed the white stone steps that led into many of Baltimore's houses. For every set of steps she washed down, she got a nickel. She needed to earn more money, however, so she began bringing along her own bucket, soap, and rags. From then on, she charged her customers 15 cents, arguing that she provided her own supplies. Even after the price hike, people hired her eagerly. Because she was big for her age and large-boned, they thought she would be a hard worker. Billie proved them right. On an average day, she earned 90 cents; on a good day, $2 or more.

*While Holiday was growing up, Hollywood actress Billie Dove was her favorite movie star. "I don't think I missed a single picture Billie Dove ever made," Holiday said. "I was crazy for her. I tried to do my hair like her and eventually I borrowed her name."*

In addition to cleaning steps, Billie did chores for Alice Dean, a local brothel owner. The youngster did some housework and ran errands for the prostitutes who worked there. But she did not receive money as payment for her work. Dean's house had a parlor with a Victrola and a stack of jazz records featuring such artists as cornetist Louis Armstrong and blues singer Bessie Smith. Jazz was just beginning to emerge as the nation's first highly popular black art form, and Billie loved this new style of music. She worked for free just so she could play the records again and again, singing along with Smith's big, earthy voice and moving in time to Armstrong's high-spirited, soulful solos, which distracted her from her surroundings and gave her a bit of joy.

*When Holiday was 10 years old, she moved with her mother to this street, Pennsylvania Avenue, in Baltimore. "We were going to live like ladies and everything was going to be fine," Billie said. But her mother found few good job opportunities in the city, and two years later they were compelled to move again.*

In 1925, Billie's mother returned to Baltimore with enough money to buy a house on Pennsylvania Avenue, in the northern part of the city. Shortly thereafter, she took a new husband, a neighborhood dockworker named Philip Gough. For a brief time, Billie had a real family again. But when Gough died suddenly, Billie knew that her mother would soon head north again in search of work.

Around this time, Billie went through

another agonizing experience. While she was coming home from school one afternoon, a neighbor grabbed her and tried to rape her. She screamed and fought back, making enough noise to draw the police, who promptly arrested her 40-year-old attacker. The police also insisted that Billie come with them to the station. "They wouldn't let my mother take me home," she said later. "They threw me into a cell. My mother cried and screamed and pleaded but they just put her out of the jailhouse."

Two days later, when the case was brought to court, the judge sentenced Billie's assailant to five years in jail. Then he ordered that the 10 year old be confined to an institution for wayward girls until she reached the age of 21—a much longer term than was given to the man who had tried to rape her. Because Billie appeared to be much older than she actually was, the judge had presumed that her mature looks had brought on the assault.

Sadie Holiday could do little to help her daughter. She had tried to give Billie a new home, but the legal system and the death of her second husband prevented that from happening. Heartbroken, she returned to the North, where she again worked as a maid for well-off families and waited for the day when her daughter would be released.

Billie loathed the institution, which was

basically a reform school for girls who were mainly truants or shoplifters. It was headed by nuns who believed in strict discipline for the girls in their custody. Students who misbehaved had to wear a torn red dress as punishment. As Holiday recounted, "When you wore this dress, none of the other girls were supposed to go near you or speak to you."

On one occasion, the sisters punished Billie by making her put on the torn dress. Then they told her she could not sleep in the dormitory with the other girls. Instead, she had to spend the night locked in a room with the corpse of a fellow classmate that the nuns had laid out for burial. Trapped in a room with a corpse close by, Billie, who could only think of her great-grandmother dying in her arms, began to panic. "I screamed and banged on the door, so I kept the whole joint from sleeping," she recalled. "I hammered on the door until my hands were bloody."

When Billie's mother heard about the incident, she became determined to remove her daughter from the institution. Aided by one of the wealthy families that employed her, Sadie managed to get the judge's ruling reversed. Billie, at the age of 12, was allowed to leave the reform school.

Deciding that both of them had had enough of Baltimore, Sadie promptly made arrange-

ments for her daughter to join her in New York. On a summer day in 1927, Billie went to the local train station and, with a basket of fried chicken to keep her occupied, made the long journey north. She was filled with high hopes for a new life.

Yet Billie's early years in New York were much like her ones in Baltimore. She took a job as a domestic, but it did not work out. Her mother, realizing that her daughter would "never make it as a maid," decided to let her board in a large Harlem apartment owned by a woman named Florence Williams. Unbeknownst to Billie's mother, Williams turned out to be a well-known madam who ran a brothel out of her apartment.

"In a matter of days I had my chance to become a strictly twenty-dollar call girl," Holiday later claimed, "and I took it." In the late 1920s, job opportunities for women were scarce; for black women, they were almost nonexistent. Billie could earn more from one customer than she could make in a month working as a maid.

*Cornetist Louis Armstrong's unique brand of music had a profound effect on Holiday's growth as a singer. One of the most influential figures in jazz history, he devised a new style of play, solo improvisation, and a novel type of singing, scat.*

It was not long, however, before the ugly side of the profession surfaced. One client almost killed Billie, prompting her to refuse another man who happened to be an extremely influential figure in the Harlem underworld. Using his leverage with the police, this man had Billie arrested "not for anything I did," she said, "but for something I wouldn't do."

In court, Billie's mother swore that her daughter was 18 years old (although she was actually no more than 13) to protect her from another long reform school sentence. Billie served time for her "offense" at an adult correctional institution on Welfare Island (now Roosevelt Island), located in New York's East River. Although conditions at the facility were grim, she took solace in knowing she had to stay there for only four months instead of spending several years in reform school.

Upon being released from prison, Billie again worked as a prostitute. But she did not remain one for long. Extremely strong willed, she refused to settle for the life she had known up to that point. "I figured there had to be something better," she maintained.

But things just kept getting worse. In 1929, Billie moved with her mother to an apartment on 139th Street, in the heart of the New York City district known as Harlem. Originally a wealthy white suburb of Manhattan, Harlem underwent a radical change in the late 1800s, when elevated railroad lines were extended into the area. The trains linked Harlem to the rest of Manhattan and prompted investors to buy up land and construct buildings at a furious pace. As a result, Harlem property values rose sharply.

The situation began to change around the turn of the century, when Harlem became overdeveloped and the housing boom collapsed, causing real estate prices to plummet. Blacks, long accustomed to living in tenements, seized the opportunity to move into attractive apartments with affordable rents. Indeed, they gravitated to Harlem from all over the country, and by 1920 it was a bustling black community, a city within a city. According to the clergyman Adam Clayton Powell, Sr., Harlem "became the symbol of liberty and the Promised Land to Negroes everywhere."

Like most black Americans, Billie longed to live in this center of opportunity, which boasted the largest urban concentration of blacks in the United States. It had also emerged as an intellectual and artistic meeting ground for blacks, and the participants in this Harlem Renaissance were the first group of American artists to praise black culture and promote black values. But the neighborhood where Billie resided in Harlem hardly seemed like a cultural paradise or a refuge from hard times. Just when she arrived there with her mother, the Great Depression began.

The effects of poverty soon became visible throughout the black community where Billie lived. What had once been one of New York's most beautiful areas began to deteriorate as tenants unable to pay their rents were forced out of their apartments and chased onto the streets. With almost half of the district's

residents out of work, the city of dreams was rapidly disintegrating into an urban nightmare.

Billie was among those who urgently needed a job. When her mother fell ill and became unable to work, they found themselves without

*Holiday and her mother moved to 139th Street in Harlem, the most celebrated black community in the country, in 1929, just as the Great Depression began to take hold. According to Billie, "A depression was nothing new to us, we'd always had it."*

enough money to buy food, let alone pay the rent. One evening, they received a notice that they were to be evicted the next morning. "I told Mom I would steal or murder or do anything before I'd let them pull that," Holiday recalled. Hungry and scared, she headed out into the cold night, determined to raise the rent money, perhaps as a dancer.

*From 1919 to 1933, when Prohibition laws were in effect, speakeasies such as the one shown here provided both illicit alcohol and live entertainment. In 1930, Holiday landed her first singing job at a Harlem speakeasy called Pod's and Jerry's.*

Billie turned the corner onto Seventh Avenue and began to walk downtown. Along the avenue for several blocks stretched a succession of restaurants, cafés, and illicit bars called speakeasies. Prohibition laws were then in effect, making the sale of liquor illegal, and speakeasies had become part of an intricate black market for alcohol. Billie went "busting

into every joint trying to find a job," she said. But every place she tried, the manager told her there was no work available.

Then Billie stopped in front of a speakeasy called Pod's and Jerry's, a basement room at West 133rd Street. It was named for its owners, Charles "Pod" Hollingsworth and Jerry Preston, who had established a loyal clientele by serving tasty fried chicken and showcasing talented pianists. Standing outside the club, Billie saw a dim light burning inside and heard the faint sound of a piano. For a moment, she thought of the nearby Cotton Club, renowned for its elaborate floor shows and chorus girls. She straightened herself, pushed open the door, and entered the club.

Although the room was dark and smoke filled, Billie could make out a few customers seated at makeshift tables, a group of women chatting in a corner, and a piano player toward the back of the room, picking out a few notes. As the door squeaked shut behind her, she headed toward the bar. All eyes rested on her for a moment. Then everyone returned to what they had been doing before she came in.

Billie stopped at the rail, ordered a glass of gin, and asked to see the manager. A man came over and asked what she wanted. Praying that he would believe her, the 15 year old told him she was a dancer looking to be hired.

The manager, Jerry Preston, yelled to the pianist to strike up a fast number. He wanted proof of Billie's talent.

As the music began, the teenager realized that her bluff had been called. "I danced the same step for fifteen choruses," Holiday later said. Obviously, she was not a dancer.

Preston was about to tell Billie to stop wasting his time when the pianist, a man named Dick Wilson, took pity on her and yelled, "Well, then, can you sing?" Billie nodded. She had been singing all her life. She had never thought, however, that she could make any money as a singer. She told Wilson to play a sad, medium-tempo number called "Trav'lin' All Alone," which was a popular song at that time. Holiday later said it "came closer than anything to the way I felt."

When the first few notes sounded from the piano, Billie started singing. By the middle of the song, everyone else in the room had grown quiet. Only the piano chords and Billie's heartfelt vocals hung in the air.

As the song came to an end, Billie held the last note. All eyes were once again upon her. But this time some were filled with tears. Billie did not understand why the people were crying. They must be feeling sorry for me, she thought. Then some of the listeners began to applaud, and others started throwing money on the floor in front of her. The people in Pod's and Jerry's had never before heard singing that was so believable and moving. Neither had Jerry Preston. He offered Billie a singing job on the spot, for a few dollars each night plus tips. She was to start right away.

That same night marked her first performance as a professional singer. Billie raked in more than $100 in tips. After splitting the money with the pianist, she stopped to buy a chicken and some baked beans for dinner, then raced home with the food to tell her mother that they could now pay the rent and afford

a square meal. Their problems—for the moment, anyway—were solved.

As excited as Billie was by her good fortune—the teenager laughed and whooped as she told Sadie again and again how frightened she had been—she was probably not thinking too far ahead. But that night, in a little speakeasy in Harlem, her singing career had officially begun.

*As the Great Depression took hold of Harlem in the early 1930s, many of the district's residents sought to forget about their troubles by taking in the local nightlife. Entertainment spots ranged in size from basement speakeasies to the Lafayette Theater (shown here), one of Harlem's most popular musical stages.*

── Chapter Three ──

# Rising
# Star

HARLEM WAS JUST reaching its
height as a musical and theatrical center when
Billie Holiday launched her career as a vocalist
in 1930. Most of the black actors, dancers, and
musicians who had made names for
themselves on the Broadway stage and at
other New York venues now called the uptown
district their home. These performers had
been moving to upper Manhattan as early as
1910, when James Reese Europe, a prominent
orchestra leader, founded the Clef Club, a
booking agency used by more than one hun-
dred and twenty-five Harlem entertainers.

*Holiday at the start of her singing career, with saxophonists
Ben Webster (left) and Johnny Russell (right). She began working at a variety of Harlem clubs, "and everywhere I went," she
said, "something was happening."*

This influx of black artists continued through the 1920s with the arrival of job-hunting wayfarers eager to contribute to the lively scene. The writer Arna Bontemps, who came to Harlem in 1924, said shortly after settling there, "From the window of a small room in an apartment on Fifth Avenue and 129th Street I looked over the rooftops of Negrodom and tried to believe my eyes. What a city!"

Of all the performing arts, music was Harlem's specialty. Earthy blues, syncopated ragtime, and jubilant gospel were already present in Harlem by 1920. But when itinerant musicians such as Fletcher Henderson and Duke Ellington arrived there in the early part of the decade, they brought something new with them: a form of music called jazz. An amalgam of blues, ragtime, spirituals, folk music, and marches, it quickly became an uptown favorite.

Jazz was ushered into New York in the summer of 1923, when the Fletcher Henderson Orchestra debuted at the Club Alabam on 44th Street near Broadway and played a selection of dance music to an enthusiastic crowd. Although this form of music originated in other parts of the country, New York—Harlem, in particular—soon became the place where jazz musicians met and exchanged techniques. "I can tell a New Orleans band from a Chicago or St. Louis type anytime," commented Fate Marable, a Mississippi riverboat pianist of the era, "but New York, of course, doesn't have any particular style—it has everybody's way of playing."

As the new music grew in popularity in Harlem, so did the number of places where it could be heard. Jazz groups filled the bills of large theaters such as the Lafayette and the Apollo and played for thousands of dancers in such ballrooms as the Savoy. Smaller clubs, including Connie's Inn and the Cotton Club, regularly presented floor shows featuring exotic sets and lively dance routines accompanied by the hot sounds of jazz. By 1930, nightlife was flourishing in uptown Manhattan. "The world's most glamorous atmosphere," exclaimed Duke Ellington when he first saw Harlem. "It is just like the Arabian Nights."

Yet some of the Harlem night spots that featured music when Holiday first arrived in the district were neither big nor glamorous. Instead, they were dark little rooms in the basement or at the ground-floor level of apartment buildings—the kinds of places that served as speakeasies. Although they usually skimped on decor, these illegal bars often featured a pianist or singer to entertain the customers. The music never got too loud,

however, because it might have disturbed the people who lived upstairs, perhaps drawing the police.

When Prohibition was repealed in 1933, making alcohol again available to the general public, many of these speakeasies became legitimate clubs that offered music on a regular basis to continue attracting customers. Some places began presenting jam sessions,

*Connie's Inn was one of several Harlem nightclubs that initially featured black performers but admitted only white patrons. Such exclusive racial policies were abandoned, however, by the time Holiday began appearing at Connie's Inn and some of the district's other prominent venues in the mid-1930s.*

in which several musicians played together without ever having rehearsed with one another. Such spontaneous playing occasionally yielded startlingly new arrangements and compositions.

For the most part, though, these clubs remained local taverns. Many of them were clustered in the same area, near upper Seventh Avenue, and catered to a primarily—although not exclusively—black clientele. These clubs sported names such as Basement Brownie's, Mexico's, the Yea Man, and the Shim Sham, and they were where Holiday learned her craft. She worked mainly at Pod's and Jerry's but sang at other night spots when she had the chance.

The people in these clubs often saw Holiday join a group of women who took turns singing and waiting on tables. These performers were nicknamed "ups" because each of them would get up and sing for a while and then pick up the tips in an unusual manner: by clamping their thighs around the bills that the customers placed on the tables. Holiday found this practice degrading, however. She accepted only those tips that were handed to her. "Look at her, she thinks she's a lady," the other girls taunted. Holiday later noted, "That was the beginning of people calling me 'Lady.'"

Just as Holiday's demeanor caused a stir, so

did her singing. Full of expression, her versatile voice allowed her to take subtle liberties with melodies, changing them much like a jazz musician improvises on an instrument. Holiday could even sing trivial or silly song lyrics and make them sound meaningful and urgent.

Such a sophisticated approach to singing yielded a novel effect. Popular singers before her simply entertained listeners. Holiday did more. She sought to communicate with them, conveying to the audience what she knew about life through song.

The records Holiday had listened to as a child contributed greatly to the evolution of her vocal style. "I wanted Louis Armstrong's feeling and...the big volume that Bessie Smith got," she said. "But I found it didn't work with me, because I didn't have a big voice...anyway, between the two of 'em, I sort of got Billie Holiday."

Although Holiday's music was different from Armstrong's and Smith's, they were all rooted in the same musical tradition: the blues, a term that refers not only to a kind of music but also to the feeling at the heart of the music. It was first heard in America toward the end of the 19th century, although it is not known exactly how the music came to be. The blues most likely evolved from a number of different musical sources, especially the work song, in which a leader sang out a line and a group responded. African in origin, work songs were brought to America by blacks forced into slavery. These songs were improvised and passed down by several generations of slaves, who used them to establish a steady beat for their labors, whether tilling fields or chopping wood.

Another influence on the blues was the field holler, a kind of vocalization also used by slaves for singing or for passing messages (because the hollers were usually incomprehensible to white slave owners). A further component of the blues was the church hymn, European in origin but transformed by American blacks into the spiritual. The words of the spirituals, promising salvation from earthly woes, brought a sense of dignity to the blacks who sang them.

At some point after the Civil War, bits of each of these musical forms merged to create the blues, an exclusively American music born out of the black experience. It is a simple form (usually 12 bars with 4 beats in each bar) heard in songs that sometimes feature only a singer and a single instrument. In many blues songs, the first and second lines repeat, and a third line pulls the narrative along.

A kind of folk music, the blues is distinguished by its purity, vitality, and depth of

*Vocalist Bessie Smith, known as the Empress of the Blues, reached the height of her success in the mid-1920s. Her approach to music greatly influenced Holiday's own singing style.*

feeling. It allowed blacks the opportunity for expression; they could say things in blues songs they were not allowed to say anywhere else. Accompanied by a guitar or piano, these people sang about everyday concerns. Although some of the tunes were often fast and comic, the best-known songs were slow and sad, and dealt with misfortune. Poverty, infidelity, loneliness, and death were subjects commonly used in blues lyrics because singing about suffering seemed to ease the pain a little. The blues song, like its cousin, the spiritual, was about deliverance.

Freed slaves, often featuring the blues in minstrel shows that traveled across America, spread the music throughout the United States. As time went on, blues songs began to reflect changes in black life. There was urban as well as country blues, and cities as far apart as New Orleans and Chicago featured different kinds of blues. The music eventually played an important part in the evolution of jazz as well as other forms of popular music, including rhythm and blues, rock and roll, and soul. Similarly, the simplicity of the blues form allowed a number of different-styled singers— including Leadbelly, Muddy Waters, and Joe Williams—to come forward and excel.

The peak of popularity for the blues was in the early 1920s, after a woman named Mamie

Smith recorded a song called "Crazy Blues." Released in 1920, the record sold more than a half million copies and began a blues craze during which a number of black female blues singers made records, including Ma Rainey and her protege, Bessie Smith, one of Holiday's early favorites. Playing trumpet on many of these first blues records was Louis Armstrong, who ultimately became a jazz pioneer by taking the spirit of the blues and, improvising on his horn, turning it into something revolutionary.

Holiday did something similar, but with singing. She was never a blues singer in the traditional sense. In fact, she resisted being categorized as one. "If they have to give me a label," she said, "call me a jazz singer." In her entire repertoire, there are fewer than a dozen actual blues songs (although two of them, "Fine and Mellow" and "Billie's Blues," are among her best-known and most popular works); the rest of her vocals sounded quite different from blues singing. Nevertheless, she brought a blues feeling—not just sadness but honesty and directness of expression—to everything she sang. Like the best blues artists, she took misery and transformed it into something different, something that stood apart from trouble and pain.

Holiday's unique, blues-inspired jazz singing

commanded attention right from the start. One night in 1933 when she was appearing at Monette's, a club on 133rd Street, John Hammond walked into the room. An avid fan of jazz and blues, he frequently made the trek uptown to Harlem to catch the latest sounds. Only 22 years old, he had already begun to establish himself as a music promoter and producer by befriending a number of musicians and writing about jazz for several European publications. (At that time, few American publications carried articles about jazz.)

At Monette's, Hammond expected to hear Monette Moore, a singer as well as the club's owner. She had just got a part in a Broadway show, however, and had booked Holiday as her temporary replacement. Hammond immediately recognized Holiday's enormous talent when she came out and sang "Wouldja for a Big Red Apple?" As she moved from table to table, he sat transfixed. "To my astonishment," he said, "she sang a completely different chorus to the same tune at each table. It was the first really improvising singer that I had heard." By the end of the evening, Hammond (who would later help launch the careers of such diversely talented artists as Benny Goodman, Count Basie, Bob Dylan, Aretha Franklin, and Bruce Springsteen) thought that "she was the best jazz singer I

*Music producer and promoter John Hammond was instrumental in launching Holiday's career. "She sang popular songs in a manner that made them completely her own," he said years after he had first heard her perform at a Harlem night spot in 1933. "She had an uncanny ear, an excellent memory for lyrics, and she sang with an exquisite sense of phrasing."*

had ever heard."

In one of his columns, in an English music magazine called *Melody Maker*, Hammond gave Holiday her first rave review. He also brought many influential people from the music and entertainment worlds uptown to hear her. One was Joe Glaser, Louis Armstrong's manager, who was so impressed by Holiday that he agreed to manage her. Clarinetist Benny Goodman, who soon became one of the most popular jazz bandleaders in the country, also accompanied Hammond to Monette's one evening. Goodman was as impressed by Holiday as Hammond had been, and together they made arrangements for her to cut a record.

The recording date was set for November 27, 1933, with Goodman assembling a nine-piece band for the occasion. Unlike today, vocalists were not at the forefront of the popular music scene—instrumentalists claimed a much larger following. Consequently, Holiday was scheduled to sing only a few choruses on the recording of "Your Mother's Son-in-Law." Nevertheless, she began to panic when she arrived at the recording studio and saw the microphone. "I'd never sung in one and I was afraid of it," she said later.

Pianist Buck Washington, formerly a member of the popular Buck and Bubbles song and dance team, realized how frightened Holiday was and went over to her. "Don't let all these white folks see you scared," he whispered in her ear. "They'll be laughing at you."

According to Holiday, "That did it." When the time arrived for her to sing a few choruses, she braced herself, walked to the microphone, and performed without a hitch. Twelve days later, the band reassembled in the studio to record the flip side, "Riffin' the Scotch." Holiday turned in fair renditions on both songs, although she later joked about them. "It sounds like I'm doing comedy," she said. "My voice sounded so high and funny." Paid about $35 for the job, Holiday was unenthusiastic and unimpressed by her first record, which did not sell very well.

Holiday returned to the clubs after her first trip to the recording studio. She sang at the Alhambra Grill and then at the Hot-Cha Bar and Grill, where Ralph Cooper, a master of ceremonies at the Apollo Theater, saw her. Cooper raved about Holiday to his boss, Ralph Schiffman, who owned the Apollo. "You never heard such singing," he told Schiffman. "It ain't the blues—I don't know what it is, but you've got to hear her." Willing to take a chance, Schiffman went to see for himself. He was equally impressed by Holiday and booked

her for a week at his theater.

As delighted as Holiday was by the upcoming engagement, she was also petrified by it. The Apollo Theater was the undisputed capital of the black entertainment world—a place where careers were sometimes made, other times ruined. Boasting the city's toughest audience, the Apollo had a rowdy atmosphere. When the theatergoers did not like a performer, they would not hesitate to boo him or her off the stage.

Schiffman had scheduled Holiday's first Apollo show for April 19, 1935, just a few days

*Clarinetist Benny Goodman (center), one of the first white bandleaders to employ black musicians, was also responsible for getting Holiday the opportunity to make her first record. Billie sang a few choruses on the disc "Your Mother's Son-in-Law," which was released in late 1933.*

after her 20th birthday. Just before she was to go onstage, she was struck with stage fright. Dressed in a satin gown and slippers, she waited in the wings of the theater, unable to keep still. Then she heard the band playing the introduction to her first number. She turned impulsively and started to hurry away. But Pigmeat Markham, a comedian also on the bill, saw what she was doing and grabbed her. He wound up pushing Holiday onto the stage and into the spotlight.

"My knees were shaking so bad the people didn't know whether I was going to dance or sing," Holiday recalled. A woman in the front row yelled, "Look, she's dancing and singing at the same time." But Holiday calmed herself, and by the time she finished her second number, she had won over the crowd. "They didn't ask me what my style was,. . .where I'd come from, who influenced me, or anything," she said. "They just broke the place up." By the end of her week-long engagement, she radiated confidence. Knowing he had come upon an extraordinary talent, Schiffman immediately booked her to play another week in August.

A few months after her first stint at the Apollo, Holiday went back into the studio—this time with happier results. The recording session, organized once again by Hammond, took place at the Brunswick Studios in midtown. Hammond engaged Teddy Wilson, a

*Holiday made her first appearance at the Apollo Theater, one of Harlem's most prestigious—and toughest—showplaces, in April 1935. After hesitating to go onstage, she easily won over the boisterous crowd and was thus on her way to establishing herself at the forefront of the jazz scene.*

brilliant young pianist from Austin, Texas, to lead the band, and arranged for Goodman to play clarinet. Hammond wanted the mood to be relaxed, like it was at a jam session or in a Harlem nightclub, so he booked the studio for late in the afternoon, when the performers were usually more at ease. This strategy ultimately paid off, as the four songs recorded were considered a great success.

Less than a month later, Holiday returned to the studio to record again with Wilson and a few other musicians. These sessions marked the beginning of a routine that she followed for the next several years. From time to time, seven or eight musicians would gather in the studio and work out loose arrangements under Wilson's direction. Holiday would listen to them rehearse and learn her part. "Those sessions were sheer joy," Wilson recalled. "Since everyone knew he was playing with the best there was, everyone on the date stimulated everybody else. That's why those records stand up so well forty years later."

Following this pattern, Holiday recorded dozens of titles (or "sides," as they were called). None of them became hit records—most sold only about 3,000 copies—yet they helped establish Holiday's reputation. The records were especially popular on the jukebox, which enabled music fans who could not afford to buy records to play them for a nickel.

During these sessions, Holiday recorded many of the songs that would eventually be associated with her, including "I Cried for You," "Mean to Me," "My Man," and others. As she kept making records, her voice improved. The impeccable musicianship of the players who accompanied her—including Wilson, trumpeter Roy Eldridge, saxophonist Ben Webster, and many others—helped inspire her. They were some of the finest players in jazz history, and she learned a great deal about music from them. "How casually we were able to assemble such all-star groups," Hammond said. "It simply was a Golden Age; America was overflowing with a dozen superlative performers on every instrument."

Neither Holiday nor her fellow musicians were paid very much for their work. But the quality of the records produced at these sessions suggests that they must have enjoyed playing together very much. Full of energy, enthusiasm, and grace, the songs produced at the Holiday-Wilson sessions formed the foundation of Holiday's reputation and are still considered some of the greatest jazz recordings ever made.

First and foremost, though, the records meant work and money. In addition to the recording sessions Holiday attended in July

1935, she performed at the Hot-Cha Bar and Grill right before her second booking at the Apollo Theater. At one of the shows, her father dropped into the club to hear her sing. They had maintained contact over the years despite having a tense relationship. She could not completely forgive him for deserting the family, and he was somewhat resentful that she had become a performer but had never asked him to back her on guitar.

That night at the Hot-Cha, however, they had a reconciliation. Clarence wanted only to congratulate his daughter and wish her well. Impressed that she was scheduled for a return engagement at the Apollo Theater, he felt that she could now play any venue in New York.

Holiday began her second engagement at the Apollo on August 2, 1935, and once again enjoyed a very successful run. By the age of 20, she had shown Harlem what she could do. The rest of the world was next.

---

*Pianist Teddy Wilson's studio sessions with Holiday resulted in some of her finest records, including "I Cried for You," which was among the first of her discs to reach a large audience.*

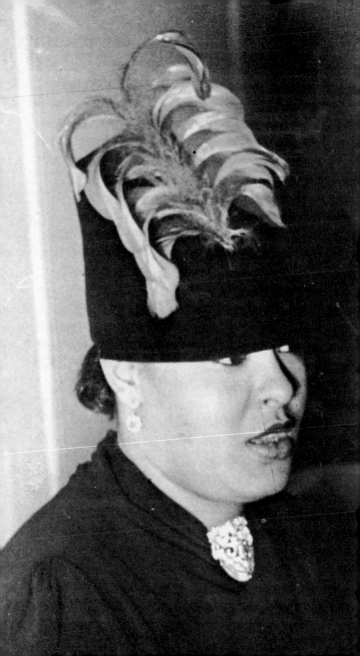

# Chapter Four

# Lady Day

BILLIE HOLIDAY'S CAREER proceeded steadily during the mid-1930s. At a studio session on July 10, 1936, she recorded "Summertime" and "Billie's Blues"—her very first discs without Teddy Wilson—and released them under her own name. The credit on each platter read: by Billie Holiday and Her Orchestra. Over the next few years, she continued to release records on the Vocalion label that cost 35 cents. When she cut records that billed Wilson as the bandleader, they were issued on the Brunswick label and sold for a much higher price, 75 cents, because he was

*Billie Holiday arrives at a studio for a recording session. According to composer Charles Fox, she "lived on the edge of every song she sang."*

a better-known artist.

In addition to making records, Holiday played a small part in a radio soap opera and appeared in a short musical film, *Symphony in Black*. She had mixed feelings about the movie, which she made in 1935 with Duke Ellington and His Orchestra. "It gave me a chance to sing a song—a real weird and pretty blues number. That was the good thing about the part," she said. "The rough part, of course, was that I had to play a chippie [prostitute]." When she said rough, she meant it quite literally. The role called for her to be knocked down on a sidewalk, and the numerous takes that the scene required left her badly bruised.

By the mid-1930s, Holiday was well known enough to play any club in Harlem. But her career was not without its setbacks. Problems tended to occur when she tried to sing for audiences outside Harlem, where some listeners thought her vocal style was not jazzy enough. In September 1935, for instance, she was fired from a show at the Famous Door Club in midtown Manhattan when the clientele failed to respond to her. One critic said, "She sings as if her shoes were too tight." On another occasion, in June 1936, she was dismissed from an engagement at the Grand Terrace Cafe in Chicago because the manager thought she sang "too slow."

There were other difficulties as well. In 1936, Holiday was hired to sing in a revue called "Stars over Broadway," which was

*Holiday in a still from* Symphony in Black, *a short film that was made in 1935 as a vehicle for Duke Ellington and His Orchestra. She had a small role in the movie, singing just a dozen bars.*

staged at Connie's Inn on 48th Street and costarred Louis Armstrong and the Luis Russell Orchestra. She had to drop out of the show shortly after it opened, however, because she contracted ptomaine poisoning. Later, in September of that same year, she appeared at the Onyx Club on 52nd Street as the opening act for Stuff Smith, a jazz violinist, who had her fired because he resented that she drew more applause than he did.

Extremely sensitive, Holiday could be temperamental and volatile about such setbacks. After being fired from the Grand Terrace Cafe in Chicago, she threw an inkwell at the club manager's head. More often, though, she took refuge in her home life. The steady work she had been receiving had enabled her to help her mother start a restaurant, and the two of them lived in the apartment above it. As a result, their home life often resembled a nonstop party. "It was," Billie said, "a combination YM-CA, boardinghouse for broke musicians, soup kitchen for anyone with a hard-luck story, community center, and after-after-hours joint where a couple of bucks would get you a shot of whisky and the most fabulous fried-chicken breakfast, lunch, or dinner anywhere in town."

Holiday loved to socialize, especially with the musicians she met at clubs, recording dates, and jam sessions in Harlem. One of her dearest friends was Lester Young, a tenor saxophonist who came east from Kansas City in 1936 with Count Basie's big band. She met Young on January 25, 1937, shortly after he arrived in New York and played at one of her recording sessions with Wilson. Born in Mississippi, Young played saxophone with a style that was light and cool—markedly different from the rich, heavy tone that was then in vogue. Eventually acknowledged as a jazz original, Young was as unique and influential a player as Holiday was a singer.

Holiday and Young hit it off immediately. They became friends and soul mates, musicians perfectly in tune with one another. "They thought alike and they felt alike," recalled John Hammond. "It was so subtle and so close that I feel embarrassed even *talking* about it." Along with trumpeter Buck Clayton, another Basie band member who played on Holiday's records, they would go out on the town, looking for a good time. They went to jam sessions, nightclubs, and house parties— "ten or twelve Harlem pads in a matter of a few hours," according to Clayton, "because [Holiday] didn't like to stay in one place too long."

After finding a rat in his hotel room, Young moved in temporarily with Holiday and her mother. As the two performers grew closer,

*Saxophonist Lester Young frequently backed Holiday's vocals on disc. Their first recording together was "I Must Have That Man," a 1937 release that revealed their remarkable understanding of each other's musical abilities.*

they gave each other nicknames. Young added *day* from Holiday to Billie's nickname, Lady, renaming her "Lady Day." And he called Sadie "Duchess" because she was the mother of a "Lady." Billie called Lester "the President," or "Pres," the commander in chief of saxophone players, and liked to joke that they were the royal family of Harlem. Concocted in fun, these nicknames have lasted to the present, and Holiday and Young are still known by these names among their fans.

Just as the temperaments of Holiday and Young were a perfect match, so was the music they made. Even Sadie said, "If I heard it from the next room, I couldn't tell if it was Pres playing or Billie humming." Trumpet player Max Kaminsky recalled that "when Lester's horn took off, Billie would just take off with him.... To hear her singing with Lester Young...was something to make your toes curl." The camaraderie between the two was also evident in the studio, and the many songs they recorded together, including "I Must Have That Man" and "Sun Showers," display a musical chemistry that places them among Holiday's finest.

Holiday said of Young, "I used to love to have him come around and blow pretty solos behind me." Accomplished horn players like Young and Clayton meshed well with all her vocal moods. On some of her recordings with them, her voice even assumes the warm and brassy quality of a trumpet or a saxophone as it dips and soars. Later in her career, she described this phenomenal ability by saying, "I don't feel like I'm singing. I feel like I am playing a horn."

On March 1, 1937, while working at the Uptown House in Harlem, Holiday received a phone call just 10 minutes before her show was about to begin. The caller informed her that her father had died of pneumonia in a Dallas hospital. His exposure to poison gas during the war had finally caught up with him, leaving his lungs too ravaged to fend off such a serious illness.

As saddened as Holiday was by this news, she became even more upset when other details about her father's death emerged. Apparently, he had got a severe chest cold while on tour with a band in Texas. Racial segregation was rigidly enforced in the South by Jim Crow laws requiring separate public facilities for blacks and whites, and Clarence had a difficult time finding a black hospital where he could receive treatment. Eventually, a veterans' hospital in Dallas agreed to take him in because he had fought in World War I. By then, however, his illness had developed into pneumonia, and he died shortly thereafter.

Holiday soon experienced southern segregation laws firsthand. Late in 1936, Hammond heard the Count Basie Orchestra's tight, blues-inspired playing on a radio broadcast and arranged for them to come east from Kansas City. He wielded considerable influence with

*Holiday with her mother, Sadie. "All she had was me," Billie said. "All I had was her."*

Basie and convinced him that the band needed a female singer to round out the act. Holiday, who had many friends in the band—including Young and Clayton as well as guitarist Freddie Greene, bassist Walter Page, and drummer Jo Jones—was just the person Hammond had in mind. When Basie heard her sing, he offered her a salary of $14 a day to join the band on tour. Anxious to travel, Holiday immediately said yes. It seemed like a perfect arrangement.

Holiday began the tour with the highest hopes. But she quickly found that life on the road was much harder than she had imagined. Most of her salary went toward food and lodging. Touring also meant many long hours spent on a bus. In the 1930s, a bus was the only economical way for a large band like Basie's to travel from city to city, and when shows were scheduled on successive days in cities up to 500 miles apart, the band had no choice but to ride all night. Even when they traveled during the day, the musicians often slept on the bus to keep from paying for a hotel room. But no matter how or where they slept, they were expected to be at their best the next day.

Confined as often as they were to the bus, Holiday and the musicians found what entertainment they could. They read, wrote letters, played music, or just talked. Occasionally, they played cards or shot dice.

One night, on their way back to New York, Holiday joined a dice game that the men were playing in the aisle of the bus. She stayed in the game for hours, as state after state rolled by. When the bus reached Manhattan, she had won more than $1,600. According to trombonist Benny Morton, "If the guys played cards Billie could play cards with them, if they shot craps, she could shoot crap. . .These people made their own fun, because they needed it. A lot of the time [they] were hurting inwardly, because the world was cruel to them."

Certainly, the hardest part of touring for the band members involved racial matters. While traveling through the Deep South, they faced the sting of the same Jim Crow laws that had plagued Clarence Holiday. Hotels, restaurants, movie theaters, and public rest rooms were all segregated according to race. Moreover, blacks were often denied admission into many musical performances. On those occasions when they were permitted inside, they had to stand behind a rope in a corner. Under no circumstances were they allowed to dance.

Racial discrimination was not any easier to bear in the North. When the Count Basie Orchestra played at Detroit's Fox Theater, a line of white female chorus dancers was featured

*In 1937, shortly after Holiday met several members of the Count Basie Orchestra, she went on tour with the band. Among her closest friends in the group were trumpeter Buck Clayton (third from left) and trombonist Benny Morton (second from right).*

with the band. As Holiday tells it, the city "was between race riots then, and after three performances the first day, the theater management went crazy." The theater owners, claiming they had received complaints that the black musicians were standing too close to the white dancers, attempted to resolve the problem by making the women in the chorus line dress up like performers in a black minstrel show.

But the orders did not stop there. The management told Holiday that she was too light skinned to sing with the band. Under the lights, they maintained, someone in the audience might think she was white. To remedy this problem, they insisted she wear special makeup to darken her complexion. Basie protested loudly, but there was little he could do about it. The band had signed a contract to perform, and so Holiday complied.

From a musical standpoint, Holiday was happy performing with the Count Basie Orchestra. But she eventually became discouraged by touring and its many hassles. Finally, in early 1938—eight months after she joined the band—they parted company.

Details about the split remain blurry. Publicly, Holiday said she quit. But in private she acknowledged that she had been dismissed. "Billie sang fine when she felt like it," said Willard Alexander of the Music Corporation of America, which managed the band. "We just couldn't count on her for consistent performance."

Holiday immediately joined another big band—a somewhat surprising turn of events given her distaste for touring. It was led by clarinetist Artie Shaw, who had played on her 1936 recording of "Did I Remember?" Like the Benny Goodman Orchestra, whose leader also played the clarinet, this band was one of the most popular groups in the country. Shaw had long admired Holiday's singing, and when he heard that she had left Basie's group, he quickly invited her to join his band.

Holiday did not jump at the chance because she knew that all the performers in the Artie Shaw Orchestra were white. An integrated band, she realized, would be even more threatening to some people than an all-black

*Holiday performing with the Count Basie Orchestra at the Apollo Theater in 1937. "The greatest thing about the Basie band of those days," she said, "was that they never used a piece of music, still all sixteen of them could end up sounding like one great big wonderful sound."*

group. Such an arrangement could only generate problems. But when Shaw told her he was determined to make the situation work, she agreed to his offer.

With Holiday in tow, trouble began plaguing Shaw's band right away. In the South, especially, an integrated group was viewed with suspicion and distaste. "It wasn't long before the roughest days with the Basie band began to look like a breeze," Holiday said about her travels with the Artie Shaw Orchestra. "Eating was a mess, sleeping was a problem, but the biggest drag of all was a simple little thing like finding a place to go to the bathroom." There were arguments, even fistfights, in some places. Holiday recalled "months of being bugged by sheriffs, waitresses, hotel clerks and crackers of all kinds in the South. Almost every day there was an incident."

On one occasion, band members used their wits to thwart Jim Crow. Before attempting to book rooms in a segregated hotel, they painted a red dot on Holiday's forehead. "Two guys carried her bags," Shaw recalled. "She got the room, not as a black or a colored person, but as an Indian."

But for all his good intentions, Shaw was unable to make Holiday's life with the band any easier, and the situation finally came to

*Clarinetist Artie Shaw (second from left) realized that in-*
*tegrating his band by having Holiday join the group would*
*create many problems. "I can take care of the situation," he*
*said. "And I know Lady can take care of herself."*

a head. In October 1938, the orchestra was scheduled to headline at the Lincoln Hotel in New York City. The hotel's management, eager to avoid upsetting its white guests, insisted that Holiday walk through the kitchen to get to the stage, use the service elevator instead of the one used by hotel guests, and wait in a small room upstairs to sing rather than sit onstage with the rest of the band.

These restrictions were more than Holiday could bear. In the South, she begrudgingly accepted racial segregation. But to be subjected to such vile decrees in her hometown was intolerable. Shortly after this incident took place, Holiday left Shaw's band. "I'll never sing with a dance band again," she told a reporter for *Down Beat*. Touring may have given her the opportunity to be heard by audiences all over the country, but that did not take away the sting of discrimination.

Holiday did not have long to brood, however. Almost immediately, Barney Josephson, a 36-year-old shoe salesman from New Jersey, offered her the opportunity to perform at a place where she would be treated with dignity and respect. Josephson wanted to establish a truly integrated nightclub, where black and white musicians could play on the same stage and black and white patrons could sit together. Although different races sometimes mingled in Harlem clubs, the idea of a mixed nightclub in other parts of Manhattan was still a radical notion. But Josephson was determined to see his dream realized.

Goodman, Hammond, and others invested money in Josephson's dream, thus enabling him to rent a basement room at 2 Sheridan Square, in the heart of Greenwich Village. He installed lights and a stage, put in about 220 seats, and had several artists paint colorful murals on the walls. As a final touch, he had matchbooks printed with the slogan, "The wrong place for the right people," on the cover. The club, known as Café Society, hoped to attract a very liberal audience.

Seeking advice about what performers to book, Josephson turned again to Hammond, who quickly recommended Holiday and several other acts. Finally, on December 28, 1938, Café Society opened its doors. Holiday was an immediate sensation. Most of the clientele had never heard a singer like her before, and their enthusiastic response was instrumental in transforming her into a star.

Holiday wound up staying at Café Society for nine months, doing three shows a night. One night a customer named Lewis Allen, who was a poet and schoolteacher, showed her a poem he had written. The poem, entitled "Strange Fruit," was a protest against racial

*Holiday in 1938, when she was performing with the Artie Shaw Orchestra. In joining the group that spring, she became one of the first black vocalists to be a member of a white jazz band.*

brutality. The words describe lynchings in the South, and the strange fruit of the title refers to the bodies of lynched blacks hanging from the branches of a tree. Holiday was moved by the poem and, with the help of Sonny White, her accompanist at the time, she adapted it into a song.

Allen's powerful imagery made "Strange Fruit" one of the most solemn and startling songs ever written. At first, Holiday was hesitant about performing it. But then she relented. She still felt bitter about the circumstances that had led to her father's death, and it was easy to recall the many times that she had encountered racial prejudice while on tour. "I'm a race woman," she once said, and "Strange Fruit" enabled her to express this sentiment to her audiences.

Holiday introduced the intensely emotional song into her act with some trepidation. "The first time I sang it I thought it was a mistake," she said. "There wasn't even a patter of applause when I finished. Then a lone person began to clap nervously. Then suddenly everyone was clapping."

Over the course of several evenings, Josephson witnessed the song's effect on the audience and felt it fit right in with Café Society's liberal atmosphere. He insisted that Holiday close each show with "Strange Fruit."

When the moment for the song arrived, table service would be suspended and all the lights in the club would be turned out except for a pin spotlight on Holiday. She would keep her eyes closed during the song's long, instrumental introduction. Then, full of emotion, she would begin to sing.

"There were no encores after it," Josephson recalled. "My instruction [to Holiday] was walk off, period. People had to remember 'Strange Fruit,' get their insides burned with it."

After performing the song regularly through the early spring, Holiday decided to make a record of "Strange Fruit." Her record company thought it too provocative a song, however, and refused to release it. To make amends, they gave her legal permission to record it for another company. So, on April 20, 1939, just a few days after her 24th birthday, Holiday cut the song for the Commodore label, which belonged to Milt Gabler, owner of the Commodore Music Shop in midtown Manhattan. A big fan of Holiday's, he often attended her shows at Café Society. "There was no sense in going home without hearing Lady," he used to say.

Gabler distributed the discs from his shop, and "Strange Fruit" immediately became Holiday's best-known record. She called it her "personal protest." But it was much more than that. "Strange Fruit," as sung by Holiday, became one of the most powerful pleas for black rights that had yet been made.

Shortly after Gabler released the song, all of New York seemed to know of Billie Holiday. "I became a celebrity," she said, then added, "When that happens, watch out."

*Holiday recording "Strange Fruit" in April 1939 with Frankie Newton. The controversial song, which she performed with heartfelt emotion, brought about a significant change in her reputation as a vocalist.*

CLUB
SAMOA
FUNK

CHING NO 1 BOY !

ELMER SNOWDEN
ORCH

THE
FAMOUS DOOR

NEMO BOYER WALSH

CLUB SAMOA

THE FAMOUS DOOR

MINSKY'S
"51" CLUB

# Chapter Five

# Good
# Times

THE SUCCESS OF "Strange Fruit" signaled a change in direction for Billie Holiday's music. Because of the slow, intense way she performed the controversial song, she was soon characterized as a serious dramatic singer. The style won her new fans, and she began to sing in this manner more frequently in her shows as well as on records. She gradually gained a reputation for being a torch singer, a performer of sentimental songs about heartbreak and unrequited love.

Some of her fans objected to this change in Holiday's style, chief among them John Ham-

*Lined with nightclubs, 52nd Street (often referred to as Swing Street) was the heart of the New York jazz scene from 1940 to 1945. Holiday established herself as the most sought-after vocalist on the club circuit during that time.*

mond, one of her earliest and most enthusiastic supporters. He acknowledged that the "shock value [of Strange Fruit] helped her career" but believed that overly dramatic songs limited her as a vocalist. Whereas her singing used to be spontaneous and versatile, it was now self-conscious and mannered. Her sparkle, it seemed to Hammond, had been replaced by heaviness. "In many ways I think the song hurt Billie as an artist," he said.

Other people felt differently. Although "Strange Fruit" prompted Holiday to alter her style somewhat, her talent remained intact, and her appeal increased steadily. The years immediately following her appearances at Café Society—the early 1940s—saw her achieve the peak of her popularity. Her records, though still not hits, sold well, and her income rose significantly.

Holiday added to her reputation by performing regularly in many of the clubs on 52nd

*Holiday taking part in a jam session in 1939. She generally preferred improvisational gatherings such as this one to "complicated arrangements."*

Street between Fifth and Sixth Avenues. To most people in the entertainment world, this block was affectionately known as "the Street." It featured a number of small night spots that resembled the clubs in Harlem where Holiday had got her start. Like their uptown counterparts, the 52nd Street clubs had served as speakeasies during Prohibition and also had small rooms with tiny bandstands and bars, sometimes a kitchen, and lots of narrow tables and chairs.

Although they were hardly fancy, the crowded rooms offered plenty of atmosphere. "The clubs were dark and smoky," jazz writer Whitney Balliett said, "the liquor was bad but cheap, and they smelled like abandoned caves. But they were the perfect places to hear jazz."

In some ways, the clubs were like a piece of Harlem transported downtown, for the most prevalent sound on 52nd Street was jazz, much of it played by black musicians. There was one main difference, though, between 52nd Street and Harlem: When the midtown clubs began featuring music in the 1930s, they were off limits to black customers—just like the more exclusive Harlem clubs had been in the 1920s.

Eventually, these racial restrictions were eased somewhat. The opening of Café Society and the debut of Benny Goodman's integrated trio, which featured Teddy Wilson, caused the exclusive policies of the 52nd Street clubs to change. According to historian Arnold Shaw, the Street embodied "the struggle of black singers and musicians to gain their rightful place in white society. . .[It] provided employment and a showcase for their talents, opening its doors a little more quickly than the rest of Manhattan's midtown restaurants, hotels, theaters and even movie palaces."

The 1940s were the heyday of 52nd Street. It became popularly known as Swing Street as well as simply the Street. Nearly twenty clubs operated on the block between Fifth and Sixth Avenues. Some, such as Club 18, offered comedy; others, such as the Hickory House, served food. But most of the clubs featured live music. Even when the owners, names, and locations of clubs changed, the people still kept coming, packing the little rooms and overflowing onto the street.

The atmosphere along the block was as festive as it was unique. It seemed as though someone had turned the street into a giant block party. Spirited patrons made the rounds of different night spots because each club offered good music, and they wanted to hear as much of it as they could. Moving in and out of several spots, they caught one show after another.

"On warm nights, when the clubs had to keep their doors open, you'd hear one band, and after a few feet, another," songwriter Johnny Mercer recalled. "It was a crazy quilt of sounds." Because the clubs were so close to each other, some musicians headlined at one spot and played as sidemen at another club on the same night. After finishing a set at one place, they would make a hasty exit and head down the block to their next gig.

Not surprisingly, the 52nd Street clubs made a unique contribution to the development of jazz. With so many fine musicians on the block, impromptu jam sessions became a common occurrence, although the number of jazzmen involved was usually small because the tiny bandstands could not hold many people. In this give-and-take atmosphere, bebop, a form of jazz generally played by small combos and characterized by altered chords and improvised rhythmic variations, began to flourish. Eventually, bebop overtook the big band sound, which required many musicians and tight, formal arrangements.

The intimate size of the 52nd Street clubs proved to be ideal for Holiday. Backed by a pianist or small group, she captivated audiences so completely that she left them breathless. Following her successful run at Café Society, she went to Kelly's Stable in

*The intimate setting of a 52nd Street nightclub provided Holiday with an ideal place to perform. According to vocalist Joe Williams, "Lady made you feel—really feel—whatever she was singing."*

1939 and then performed at other 52nd Street haunts, including the Onyx, the Downbeat, the Spotlite, and the Yacht Club. She often headlined at these clubs for weeks.

By the early 1940s, Holiday was Swing Street's highest-paid performer, earning close to $1,000 a week. Arthur Jarwood, owner of the Famous Door, where she appeared intermittently between 1940 and 1943, said, "We didn't have to advertise. We didn't need publicity. Word got around and the club would be packed. And she was musically at her peak."

Holiday's success at the 52nd Street clubs was partly due to her becoming a torch singer. Many people identified with her songs about loneliness and lost love, especially at a time when the horrors of World War II were affecting everyone's life. "In some ways," noted Shaw, "Billie's tortured style, the sense of hurt and longing, may have been a perfect expression of what servicemen and their loved ones were feeling."

During Holiday's tenure at Kelly's Stable, Sylvia Sims, a fellow jazz singer, furnished Holiday with an accessory that was to become a lasting part of her image. One night before a performance, Holiday burned her hair with a curling iron. Sims, who was in the room with her, promptly went to a club down the street, where the coat-check girls were selling flowers. Sims bought a big white gardenia and gave it to Holiday, who wore it that night to cover the burned section of her hair. She liked wearing the flower so much that she began to put a gardenia in her hair before every performance.

Holiday performed around the country as well as at New York clubs. One of her regular stops in the 1940s was the west coast, where she became a favorite entertainer of many Hollywood stars. She also continued to make records, cutting two of her best-known songs, "Gloomy Sunday" and "God Bless the Child," in 1941.

Cowritten by Holiday, "God Bless the Child" was inspired by a visit to her mother's restaurant, Mom Holiday's, at 99th Street and Columbus Avenue. One day, when Holiday asked her mother if she could borrow some money, Sadie refused. Billie immediately became angry and muttered, "God bless the child that's got his own." The phrase stuck in her head, so she went to see composer Arthur Herzog, and they wrote a song around it. Extremely heartfelt, "God Bless the Child" became one of her biggest hits.

In 1944, Holiday decided to change record labels. She moved to Decca, where her friend Milt Gabler, who had recorded "Strange

Fruit" five years earlier, was working. On "Lover Man," her first record for Decca, she wanted to be backed by violins. In years to come, such jazz greats as saxophonist Charlie Parker and trumpeter Clifford Brown would record with strings. But in the mid-1940s, it was unusual to find such instrumentation on a jazz record. Consequently, Gabler, who was slated to produce the single, disagreed with Holiday's suggestion. They argued over the use of violins, and Holiday refused to give in and eventually won the fight.

The resulting recording of "Lover Man" proved her instincts had been correct. Thus, Holiday became, in Gabler's words, "the first black artist in her field to record with strings."

*Holiday performing in 1939 at Café Society, then the only
unsegregated night spot in New York outside Harlem. "I
opened [at] Cafe Society as an unknown," she said. "I left two
years later as a star."*

# Chapter Six

# The
# Dark Side

BILLIE HOLIDAY'S POPULARITY in the 1940s was undercut by a tragic development in her personal life. Early in the decade, she became addicted to drugs. According to Holiday, she first tried heroin, a strongly physiologically addictive narcotic, during her involvement with Jimmy Monroe, whose brother, Clark Monroe, owned the Uptown House. She contended, however, that "one had nothing to do with the other. . . Jimmy was no more the cause of my doing what I did than my mother was. That goes for any man I ever knew. I was as strong if not stronger than any

*Holiday in 1945, when her heroin addiction was no longer a secret. Nevertheless, she still wore long gloves to hide the track marks on her arms.*

of them."

But many of Holiday's friends disagreed with this opinion. She dated many men, yet they always seemed to be the wrong kind. "When it came to getting involved with a guy," said one of her friends, "her choice always seemed weird. If there was one guy in a crowded room that was tough, and mean, and meant trouble, then [she] would find him."

Monroe, it seems, was no exception. An opium smoker, he did not meet with the approval of Holiday's manager, let alone her mother. Nevertheless, Holiday married him on August 25, 1941—"to prove something" to her family and friends, she said.

Holiday began to share her husband's opium habit shortly after they were married. A little more than a year later, when the marriage began to fall apart, she began using heroin. "That's when I became hooked," she later said.

Like most drug users, Holiday thought at first that she could control her habit. The day after she first injected the drug into her veins, she told Buck Clayton, "It will make you feel like you've never felt before." He told her flatly, "No, Lady, that's not for me."

When her marriage to Monroe ended, Holiday became involved with a trumpet player named Joe Guy, another heroin addict. She increased her use of the drug, and by the mid-1940s she needed fixes every day. Because 52nd Street attracted all types of people, including drug dealers, she had little difficulty procuring heroin. "I had the white gowns and the white shoes," she recalled. "And every night they'd bring me the white gardenias and the white junk."

The dealers knew Holiday made a lot of money and charged her accordingly. It has been estimated that, at the height of her drug addiction, she spent more than $500 a week on heroin. "It wasn't long before I was one of the highest-paid slaves around," she said. "I was making a thousand a week—but I had about as much freedom as a field hand in Virginia a hundred years before."

Holiday's drug use is not hard to explain. Her difficult childhood left her emotionally scarred, extremely sensitive, and insecure. "I believe she was deceived by a lot of people," trombonist Benny Morton said, "because anyone could butter her up, saying nice things about her. She wanted to hear these things, because no grown-up seemed to love her when she was growing up."

As an adult, Holiday still seemed vulnerable. Even though she had a successful career, she was unfazed by her many accomplishments. Because her singing style was

not conventional, she never became a national sensation during her lifetime, and that troubled her. She once told a writer that she would quit singing professionally if she did not become more popular.

The personal troubles that Holiday experienced—loneliness, prejudice, the ebb and flow of success—gnawed at her and left her discouraged and disappointed. Drugs

*Holiday at a recording session in 1940. Although she was widely admired by other vocalists and jazz musicians, her failure to produce a hit song left her deeply troubled.*

countered those feelings. They made her numb and helped her forget her dissatisfaction.

Though Holiday's drug use can be explained, it is hard to comprehend. She possessed enormous talent and was loved by many. Friends and fans alike applauded her every night. Yet she was unable to let their adoration ease her troubled heart. For reasons that are hers alone, she allowed herself to self-destruct.

The only sure thing is that once Holiday started taking heroin, she was never the same again. Each day, she had to make more and more allowances for a habit that left her physically debilitated and—despite all she earned—in constant need of money. At the peak of her career and talent, she started on a slow, downward spiral.

Holiday's situation grew more desperate in 1945, while she was on tour in Washington, D.C. She claimed that she felt her mother's spirit "come up behind me and put her hand on my shoulder." She learned the following day that her mother had died. Deeply shaken, Holiday returned to New York for the funeral.

Holiday later said that she "couldn't cry" because "wherever Mom was going it couldn't be worse than what she'd known. She was through with trouble, through with heartache, and through with pain." But Holiday's own pain was far from over. With the death of her mother, she lost the one person she loved and trusted completely. As a result, she sank deeper into despair—and drug addiction.

At first—on the outside, at least—everything seemed to be all right. In 1943, she was voted Best Vocalist in a jazz critics poll sponsored by *Esquire* magazine, and the following January she sang at a concert by the winners that was held at the Metropolitan Opera

House. Two years later, she performed at New York's Town Hall. It marked her first solo appearance in a concert hall setting. Performing eighteen songs in a little more than an hour, she delighted the audience and critics alike. Even Hammond admitted, "It was a triumph long overdue."

In 1946, while working in a Hollywood club, Holiday landed a part in a feature film entitled *New Orleans*. The movie was set in the Deep South and was supposed to be about the birth of jazz. It featured Louis Armstrong, one of her childhood idols, along with a host of other musicians.

Despite its attempt to re-create the early jazz scene, *New Orleans* proved to be little more than a flimsy romance. To make matters worse, both Holiday and Armstrong were cast as domestics. Even though blacks were rarely given the opportunity to play roles other than servants, Holiday, who had always wanted to appear in a Hollywood movie, had expected to play herself "doing a couple of songs in a nightclub setting." She was bitterly disappointed when she saw the script. "I fought my whole life to keep from being somebody's damn maid," she said. "It was a real drag to go to Hollywood and end up as a make-believe maid."

Holiday fought with her manager to get

released from the contract, but to no avail. The picture was completed, and it was released on June 9, 1947, to miserable reviews. It failed at the box office and disappeared quickly.

By then, signs of Holiday's drug addiction had begun to surface. She showed up late for

*In January 1944, Holiday and other award winners in* Esquire *magazine's first annual jazz critics' poll performed at New York's Metropolitan Opera House. The occasion marked her first appearance in a major concert hall.*

performances or missed them completely, prompting *New Yorker* magazine to call her "moody." Her drug habit even forced some club owners to act as her baby-sitter. "The problem would start after the first show," said Monte Kay, who produced shows at the Yacht

*Louis Armstrong and Holiday on the set of the film* New
Orleans *in 1946—a disappointing experience for both of them.
"They had taken miles of footage of music and scenes in New
Orleans, but none of it was left in the picture," she later said.
"I never made another movie."*

Club. "She insisted on going home. . . .Once
she was home, however, she was lost until I
went and brought her back."

Ralph Watkins, who owned Kelly's Stable,
said he never had any trouble with Holiday until she started using heroin. But from then on,
she was always trying to borrow money. Sylvia

Sims said, "It was only when she started wearing the gloves that we realized something was wrong." Holiday had begun donning elbow-length gloves to cover the needle marks on her arms.

Perhaps worst of all for Holiday was the tight grip that drugs had on her. When she did not take heroin, she became violently ill. Indeed, drug withdrawal is one of the most uncomfortable aspects of a heroin addict's life. The drug user's body seems to turn on itself until it receives another injection. The tremendous pain of going through drug withdrawal is a major reason why it is so incredibly difficult for a person to break free of a drug habit.

While on tour in California, Holiday found herself in the midst of withdrawal. She ran out of drugs and did not know of any dealers far from home. "I had to get it myself and didn't know where to begin," she said. "I was as helpless as a week-old baby left all alone in its crib, hungry and unable to do anything about it except cry. . . I cried until I was sick."

Finally, in 1947, Holiday decided to beat her habit. She checked into a New York sanatorium and spent the next three weeks there absolutely drug free. Going cold turkey under the staff's supervision seemed to do the trick. When she was released from the sanatorium, she seemed to be cured. But as soon as Holiday returned to the stage, she began taking heroin again.

Ever since Holiday's stay at the sanatorium, rumors had started to circulate about her having a drug problem. At least one of these reached the U.S. Bureau of Narcotics; several agents were soon assigned to follow her. On May 16, while she was performing at the Earle Theater in Philadelphia, federal agents raided her hotel room. Holiday heard about their search and, in a panic, fled by car to New York. But there was no place for her to hide. A few days later, narcotics agents closed in and arrested her and Joe Guy in a hotel room.

Holiday's case was brought to trial on May 27 in Philadelphia. She waived her right to an attorney and pleaded guilty to the charge of narcotics possession with the hope that the judge would send her to a rehabilitation center, where she could try once more to get off heroin. Instead, she was sent to the Federal Reformatory for Women at Alderson, West Virginia, for a year and a day. Instead of entering a hospital, she was going to prison.

*By the late 1940s, Holiday could no longer mask the effects of drug abuse. Just when she was about to reach the peak of her career, she had become an unreliable performer.*

# Chapter Seven

# Falling Star

THE ENTHUSIASTIC audience that attended Billie Holiday's Easter eve concert at Carnegie Hall on March 27, 1948, the nine and a half months that she spent in prison seemed to have done her little harm. She looked healthy (in part because she had gained back some of the weight she had lost while using drugs) and was in fine voice. But appearances were misleading. Imprisonment did considerable damage to her career—and to her state of mind. Eventually, her stay in prison was seen as the point after which her fortunes turned most sharply.

*A seemingly upbeat Holiday with her dog Mister in a backstage dressing room, following her release from prison. Happiness soon gave way to despair and she resumed her drug habit.*

Holiday's most pressing problem upon leaving Alderson was obtaining a New York City cabaret card. In order to perform at a New York City club that had a liquor license, an entertainer needed to have this permit. But because of her narcotics conviction, Holiday was denied her request for such a card. She could still sing at theaters and concert halls, but without a permit to perform in cabarets, she was legally banned from making nightclub appearances. "I can play Carnegie," she noted dryly, "but I can't play the crummiest gin joint in New York."

Forced to scrape for bookings, Holiday began to refer to herself as a DP (displaced person), the label attached to World War II refugees. Then along came Al Wilde, a producer who convinced Holiday that he could get her a gig on Broadway if he showcased her in a revue. On April 27, 1948, one month after her Carnegie Hall concert, she opened at the Mansfield Theater in a production called "Holiday on Broadway." The show received good reviews but closed after five days, in part because the Mansfield management had never before presented a jazz revue and failed to promote the show properly.

A short time later, Holiday met John Levy, who promised to do even more for her than Wilde had done. One of the managers of a New

*Holiday with dancer Bill "Bojangles" Robinson at the Ebony Club in 1948. Thanks to the influence of one of the club's managers, John Levy, she was able to perform at the New York night spot even though she was technically barred from appearing in any of the city's cabarets because of her prison record.*

York night spot called the Ebony Club, he said that he could arrange for her to sing at the cabaret without the police intervening. To get her to accept this offer, he wooed Holiday by buying her expensive gifts: a mink coat, a pea green Cadillac, jewelry, clothes; he granted her every wish. Eventually, she assented.

Levy certainly benefited from the arrangement as much as Holiday did. People flocked to her appearances at the Ebony Club as the police, probably paid off by Levy, looked the other way. As Holiday succinctly put it, "There was somebody's money behind him."

In time, Levy seemed to have absolute control over Holiday as well. She trusted him completely and put him in charge of her finances. She even began referring to him as her husband although they were not married.

When the Ebony Club closed for the summer season, Holiday found herself without a steady source of income because she lacked a cabaret card. Her manager, Joe Glaser, addressed the problem by booking her at the Strand Theater on Broadway for six weeks in July and August. The Strand, which presented films and stage shows, was not classified as a cabaret.

The theater's management put Holiday on a bill with the Count Basie Orchestra. She gave five shows a day, seven days a week, for the duration of the engagement and helped draw some of the biggest crowds in the Strand's history. Thousands came to see her—old fans as well as those whose curiosity was ignited by the publicity surrounding her arrest and imprisonment.

*In the summer of 1948, Holiday joined the Count Basie Orchestra on the bill at the Strand Theater in New York. "People were standing when the place opened in the morning," she said. "People were still standing for the last show at night."*

Yet Holiday remembered her engagement at the Strand as encompassing some of the worst days of her life. The biggest reason was her reputation as a drug addict. Because drug use in the 1940s was not as widespread as it is today, she constantly moved under a cloud of suspicion. "They come to see me get all fouled up," she said at the time. "They want to see me fail." Her already shaky self-confidence began to waver even more when she discovered that her every move was being scrutinized by the press.

Local police and federal narcotics agents also had Holiday under their watchful eye, ready to pounce on her if they spotted her using drugs. When they harassed her backstage and warned her to "watch her step," some of her friends began to shy away from her, afraid for their own reputations. Even some of the musicians who were drug users avoided her out of fear that associating with her would cause them to get busted.

Such harsh treatment began to take its toll on Holiday. "I'm tired of fighting," she had said wearily after her release from prison. "All my life it's been nothing but fighting." But her situation only grew worse, thanks to Levy. He kept the $3,500 a week she earned at the Strand. When she asked for money, he told her: "What do you need with cash? I'll give

*Holiday shortly after being arrested on narcotics charges in San Francisco on January 22, 1949. Although she was cleared of the charges several months later, the publicity surrounding her arrest and trial sent her into further decline.*

you what you need." Instead of safeguarding her earnings, he was actually keeping her income for himself—a tactic that he continued to employ when the Strand engagement ended in September and she returned to the Ebony Club.

Their relationship finally came to a head in January 1949, when Holiday and Levy were in San Francisco. A friend phoned Levy in his hotel room and told him that narcotics agents were about to bust him for drug possession. Upon hearing this, Levy handed Holiday all the opium he had and told her to get rid of it. Just then, federal agents burst into the room and arrested the two of them.

Levy quickly left town after the charges against him were dropped because there was not enough evidence to convict him. Holiday, however, had to stand trial because she was the one holding the drugs when the authorities arrived. To help clear her name, she immediately underwent a series of elaborate tests at a clinic to prove that she was not on drugs at the time of her arrest.

Holiday had maintained in a number of different interviews following her release from prison that she was "cured for good" of her drug habit. "When I was on it, I was on it," she said of heroin. "Now I'm off it, and I don't want it, and I won't have it, and that's the end of it."

But neither Holiday's statements nor the outcome of her trial could repair her public image. At the trial's conclusion in May, Holiday was exonerated. Nevertheless, the case did a lot of damage to her image. A swirl of publicity surrounded the trial, linking her once more to drugs. On top of that, she had a difficult time coming up with enough money to cover her legal fees—many of the bills Levy was supposed to have paid were still outstanding.

At the age of 35, Holiday was all alone and without much money yet again. With her mood shifting between hope and despair, she noted that her popularity continued to grow but attributed this phenomenon to her troubles as much as her talent. People came to hear her sing chiefly because she had been the subject of newspaper headlines. She stated once more, "The only reason they're out there is to see me fall into the damn orchestra pit."

As self-doubt reclaimed Holiday, she turned again to heroin to make her insecurities—and everything else that was bad in her life—go away. But her return to the drug brought back all the old problems. Heroin made her less reliable, hurt her voice, and endangered her health. "I wasn't only in awe of her singing, I was in awe of her habit," recalled Anita O'Day, a jazz singer who was also addicted to heroin. "She didn't cook up on a spoon...she used a small tuna fish can and shot 10 cc into her feet. Later...she ran out of veins."

*Holiday during a light moment backstage at the Apollo Theater with photographer Gordon "Doc" Anderson. According to pianist Hazel Scott, "There were many dimensions to [Holiday], not merely the sad-faced junkie."*

Even as Holiday's life seesawed dramatically, her strength of spirit kept her from giving up completely. As a result, the 1950s—the decade that marked her decline—also included a number of her most memorable achievements. Her talent endured in spite of the drugs, debts, and disappointments that haunted her during these years. Music sustained her, as it always had, perhaps because she knew she could trust it. "The only time she's at ease and at rest with herself is when she sings," jazz singer Carmen McRae observed.

In 1952, Holiday signed a recording contract with Norman Granz, a jazz promoter and producer who became jazz vocalist Ella Fitzgerald's manager two years later. A social reformer, Granz saw jazz as a weapon to be used in the fight for civil rights, and he helped break down racial barriers in many parts of the United States by sponsoring concerts with integrated seating. He was equally sensitive to the troubles faced by musicians and believed that Holiday should be given a chance to work regardless of her problems. "Billie Holiday was a great artist," he explained matter-of-factly. "She needed recordings, so you did them." And thus, for five years, Holiday made records under his direction.

Eventually released under the Verve label, these discs differed from the ones Holiday had been making for Decca. Instead of featuring carefully planned arrangements, Granz made sure that the Verve sessions were loosely organized. He allowed Holiday to improvise with her fellow musicians, among them Ben Webster, Freddie Greene, and Harry Edison, who had played behind her years earlier. In many ways, Granz's approach to capturing Holiday's voice on vinyl mirrored John Hammond's efforts, which had resulted in some of her finest records.

Under Granz's direction, Holiday rerecorded many of her old songs, including "Strange Fruit," "God Bless the Child," and "I Cried for You." Possessing a sad beauty, her voice on these later versions sounded dramatically different from the way it did on her earlier records. Damaged by years of hard living, it had become raspy. Her vocal range had also shrunk, and her pitch and control had become unsteady. At times, she half-spoke the lyrics instead of singing them. According to Whitney Balliett, her voice "sometimes gave the impression of being pushed painfully in front of her, like a medicine ball."

To a number of listeners, Holiday's later work was a distorted version of her earlier performances. Vastly different in mood and execution from what preceded these records, they prompted one critic to go so far as to

*Norman Granz, a music producer and promoter who worked with Holiday, was instrumental in integrating theaters and clubs and making jazz better known around the world. "It is an ideal medium for bringing about a better understanding among all peoples," he said.*

refer to her as "Lady Yesterday." Yet she had many supporters as well, including trumpeter Miles Davis, who called her later work "more mature," pointing out that the vocalist was "not thinking now what she was in 1937...She's probably learned more about different things."

Holiday also kept up a schedule of live appearances, and in 1954 she fulfilled a personal dream when she embarked on her first European tour. She had captured the attention of many music fans abroad ever since the early days of her career, and they had anxiously awaited the chance to hear her perform in person. For three weeks, she played to enthusiastic audiences in Scandinavia, Germany, Holland, Belgium, France, Switzerland, and England. The tour culminated with her triumphant appearance before a crowd of 6,000 at London's Royal Albert Hall. That concert was "the biggest thrill of my life," she said.

The constant acclaim and adoration made Holiday feel extremely confident. "The stuff they wrote about me in Europe made me feel alive" was how she put it, hinting that the American press treated her much differently. Jazz historian Leonard Feather, who had organized the tour, commented, "If Billie had had, in the formative years of her career, the kind of encouragement she received in Europe

*Holiday onstage at London's Royal Albert Hall, the last stop on her 1954 European tour. She was extremely popular abroad throughout most of her career.*

twenty years later, perhaps there might have been much more left to her voice, her morale, her life."

On occasion, Holiday still experienced gratifying moments at home. *Down Beat* presented her with a special award in 1954, calling her "one of the all-time great vocalists in jazz." On July 18 of that same year, shortly after she returned from Europe, she appeared at the first Newport Jazz Festival, which was held in Newport, Rhode Island. To the thousands of music lovers who gathered in the open air to hear some of the country's greatest artists, she sang exceptionally well. Some of Holiday's old friends played behind her during her set, including Lester Young (who was there despite being in ill health) and Teddy Wilson, who said of her performance, "I felt that the magic was there."

Holiday's personal life soon took a turn for the better, too. In 1956, she married Louis McKay, whom she had known for close to twenty years. Following their marriage, he accompanied Holiday on her tour of the United States and Europe. His presence seemed—initially, at least—to give his wife the sense of security that she had always craved. Some people went so far as to credit the relationship with giving Holiday a "new sense of responsibility and cooperativeness."

At McKay's bidding, Holiday decided to write her life story. She recounted her experiences to William Dufty, a friend of hers who worked as a journalist for the *New York Post*, and in the summer of 1956 Doubleday published the fruit of their collaboration under the somewhat ironic title *Lady Sings the Blues*—Holiday had always bristled when anyone referred to her as a blues singer. She and Dufty had wanted to call the book *Bitter Crop*.

Holiday's autobiography held back none of the brutal details of her life. It included frank accounts of her difficult childhood, her encounters with racism, and her drug addiction. It also reflected her sense of humor and her resilient spirit. The book received mixed reviews, with the stormiest reactions coming from those who knew Holiday and disagreed with her version of certain events. Leonard Feather called it "such a bizarre blend of fact, wishful thinking, rationalization, distortion and falsification that it is extremely hard, even for one who has known her. . .to determine where truth ends and fiction begins."

Although the facts in *Lady Sings the Blues* were not completely reliable, Holiday's message to her readers was unmistakably clear. "Dope never helped anybody sing better or play music better or do anything better," she

*Holiday performing at an outdoor concert. "I've been told nobody sings the word 'hunger' like I do," she said. "Or the word 'love.' Maybe I remember what those words are all about."*

wrote. "All dope can do for you is kill you—and kill you the long slow hard way." She call-ed this realization the lesson of her life.

To promote her book, Holiday gave two shows at Carnegie Hall on the night of November 10, 1956. At four different points during each show, Gilbert Millstein, a writer for the *New York Times*, read long portions from *Lady Sings the Blues* as Holiday stood in the background, her white gown barely discernible in the shadows. After he finished reciting an excerpt, she moved into the spotlight and sang several songs, then withdrew to allow him to read more of her story.

Extremely dramatic, the unusual presenta-tion gave Holiday's music added emotional weight. "Anything I do sing, it's part of my life," she once said, and these two perfor-mances proved her point. With Millstein's readings framing her songs, the audience was treated to an intimate glimpse of an excep-tional artist. "It was a night," Nat Hentoff wrote in *Down Beat*, "when Billie was on top, the best jazz singer alive."

Sadly, it was one of her last blazes of glory.

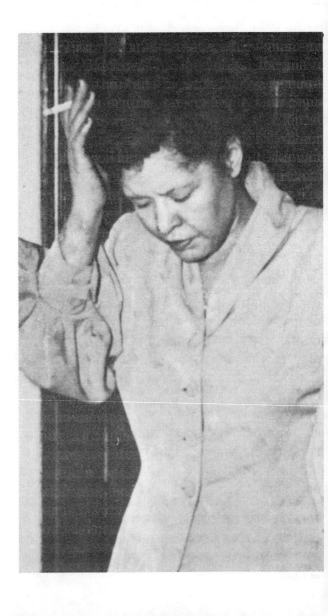

# Chapter Eight

# Billie's
# Blues

B ILLIE HOLIDAY WROTE in *Lady
Sings the Blues*, "There isn't a soul on this
earth who can say for sure that their fight with
dope is over until they're dead." These words
came from her heart and were written as her
struggle with heroin continued. On February
23, 1956, a few months before the publication
of her autobiography, police arrested her again
in Philadelphia and charged her with possession of narcotics. Her husband was also arrested for illegally possessing a firearm.

To win support for her case, Holiday returned to New York after being released on bail

*Holiday leaving a Philadelphia jail in February 1956 after be-
ing arrested yet again on drug charges. Shortly thereafter, she
agreed to enter a rehabilitation clinic to undergo treatment for
her heroin addiction, even though she felt that "with all the
doctors, nurses, and equipment, they never get near your insides
at what's really eating you."*

and entered another drug clinic. Unlike her previous attempts to overcome her drug habit, this time she did not go off heroin suddenly and completely. Instead, doctors ran a battery of tests on her and then prescribed certain drugs to help her decrease her heroin dependency gradually.

The treatment seemed successful at first. Then Holiday turned to alcohol. Like heroin, it helped her to escape reality. She did not go back to using heroin, but she was soon drinking as much as two bottles of liquor each day.

Eventually, Holiday's new method of escape put a great strain on her relationship with Louis McKay and helped destroy their marriage. For his part, Billie's husband responded to the stress by becoming violent. The couple separated in 1957, and the following year the 43-year-old singer filed for divorce, although the decree never became final.

Alone, Holiday retreated into a private hell. At her small, ground-floor apartment at 26 West 87th Street, she followed a listless routine. Evening after evening, she sat by herself for hours, drinking, smoking, watching television, and dozing for brief periods. She also doted on her dog, a chihuahua named Pepi that became her strongest emotional attachment.

By the end of the 1950s, Holiday's career

was slowing to the same sad halt as her private life. Her heavy drinking and deteriorating health made her an unreliable performer. At some shows, she appeared so drunk that she had to be helped to the microphone—an occurrence that distressed even her most loyal fans. A small item in *Down Beat* magazine plainly stated the severity of her condition. It read, "Doctors have told Billie Holiday to give up liquor or it will only be a matter of time."

Occasionally, the fog of inebriation lifted sufficiently for Holiday to work regularly. In February 1958, she began to record with Ray Ellis, an arranger who used strings as well as jazz instrumentation to create lush orchestral backgrounds for her voice. But Holiday's behavior often turned the sessions into troublesome affairs. She usually arrived at the studio around midnight, carrying a bottle of gin and a six-pack of soda, her refreshments for the night. Constantly intoxicated, she wasted a lot of studio time. The recording process took months to complete. Yet the resulting album, *Lady in Satin*, became one of her biggest sellers.

Around this time, Holiday returned twice to Europe. Although her uneven performances were poorly received, life in Europe fortified her and started her talking about taking up residence in England, where she felt appre-

Lady

ciated. But such a move never materialized.
On March 15, 1959, Holiday learned that
Lester Young had died after a long illness. She

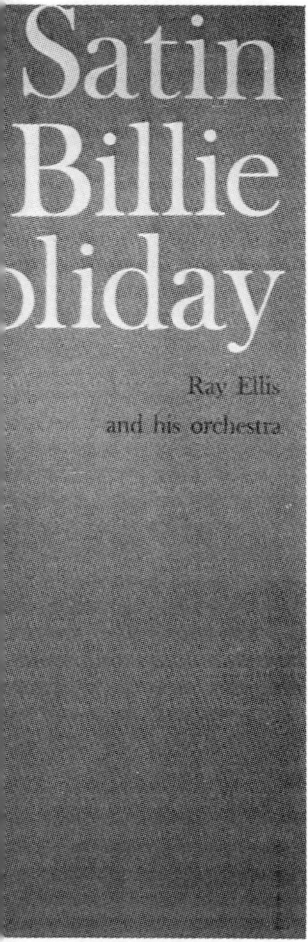

Satin
Billie
oliday

Ray Ellis
and his orchestra

Lady in Satin, *one of Holiday's last albums, was also among her most controversial recordings. The gritty tone of her voice appealed to some listeners but seemed to others a poor reminder of her former sound.*

attended his funeral with a small bottle of gin stashed inside her purse and said to friends, "I'll be the next one to go." She had last seen

*Holiday in December 1957, during the filming of a television special, "The Sound of Jazz." Her performance, which was accompanied by saxophonist Lester Young, prompted critic Nat Hentoff to say, "I felt tears and saw tears on the faces of most of the others there... This had been its climax—the empirical soul of jazz."*

Young in December 1957, when they had appeared together on "The Sound of Jazz," a special television broadcast on CBS. During the show, he had backed Holiday on saxophone, just like in the old days.

A few weeks after Young's death, Holiday celebrated her 44th birthday by throwing a small party attended by a few friends, who were struck by how well she looked. Later that April, she gave a series of performances at the Storyville Club in Boston that seemed to bear out their impression. George Wein, an organizer of the Newport Jazz Festival, was at several of the shows and said of Holiday's performances, "She was singing better than I had heard her sing in years. It was as if a miracle had happened."

Unfortunately, the miracle did not last very long. One month later, while performing at the Phoenix Theater in Greenwich Village, she had to be helped off the stage after completing two numbers. As soon as she was out of the audience's sight, she collapsed.

Leonard Feather followed Holiday into her dressing room, where she sat in a stupor. He could not hide his dismay.

"What's the matter, Leonard?" she muttered sardonically. "You seen a ghost or something?"

Holiday's show at the Phoenix was her last

public appearance.

On the afternoon of May 31, 1959, Holiday collapsed again, this time in her apartment. An ambulance took the unconscious singer to the emergency room at Knickerbocker Hospital, where she remained without treatment for over an hour. Eventually, her condition was diagnosed as being either drug or alcohol related, and she was transferred to Metropolitan Hospital in Harlem. There her personal physician, Eric Kaminer, determined that she was critically ill with cirrhosis of the liver. She was also suffering from heart failure. He ordered that she be placed immediately into an oxygen tent.

The doctor's actions helped Holiday regain consciousness and, after a few days, some of her strength. Friends visited the stricken performer in her hospital room, which began filling up with flowers and get-well cards. Louis McKay flew in from California when he heard of her illness and kept her constant company.

Then, two weeks after Holiday was first admitted to Metropolitan Hospital, she suffered a different kind of setback. On June 12, New York City detectives searched her room and claimed to have found a packet of heroin. Her doctor insisted that it was impossible for her to take narcotics at this time. It might have been planted in the room by someone, or else

*Holiday at home during her final years, when alcoholism
replaced her drug addiction.*

it might have been dropped by a visitor.

Nevertheless, the police returned to the hospital and arrested Holiday even though she was still on the critical list. They fingerprinted her and took mug shots while she lay in a hospital bed. Then they had her privileges taken away—everything from her portable record player to her candy and ice cream. To make sure nothing went amiss, a guard was stationed at her door. "Daddy," she whispered to McKay, "I didn't know they could be this cruel to nobody."

In the face of these actions, Holiday held on. As William Dufty had once observed, "She always got stronger when the going got rough." She responded well to treatment, and her condition stabilized. Then her body began to give way once again. On July 11, she developed a kidney infection that weakened her heart still further. She was ordered back into an oxygen tent.

This time there was no recovery. Her body was simply too worn down. At 3:20 in the morning on July 17, 1959, Billie Holiday died at the age of 44. The medical report listed the cause of her death as "congestion of the lungs complicated by heart failure." Jazz writer Ralph Gleason put it more bluntly when he wrote, "She had been dying by inches for years."

Indeed, Holiday's brief life was hard and sad. At times, she was a victim of society. Yet she was just as often her own worst enemy, sinking into a sea of self-destruction and despair. Some critics contend that her troubles fueled her art, helped make it darker and greater. Nevertheless, her problems, particularly her abuse of heroin and alcohol, cut short her achievements—and her life.

Hospital attendants assigned to move Holiday's body found $750 in $50 bills taped to her leg. The money, an advance payment for a magazine article she had promised to write about her life, represented nearly all she had left. In her bank account was just 70 cents. Most of her earnings had been claimed by drugs.

Several days later, more than 10,000 friends and fans went to the Universal Funeral Chapel at Lexington Avenue and 52nd Street (the same street where many of them had heard her sing) to view her body, which was laid out in pink lace. On July 31, ten policemen were needed to direct traffic as 3,000 mourners packed St. Paul the Apostle Church in Manhattan for her funeral service. Among those in attendance were Leonard Feather, John Hammond, Benny Goodman, and Teddy Wilson.

When the service was over, the funeral procession, led by three limousines and two cars

*Thousands of people attended Holiday's funeral services on July 21, 1959, at St. Paul the Apostle Church in New York. A longtime drug addict, she said shortly before her death: "All dope can do is kill you—and kill you the long slow hard way."*

filled with flowers, headed north to St. Raymond's Cemetery in the Bronx, making a slight detour along 110th Street in Manhattan to allow Holiday's body to pass through Harlem one last time. Upon reaching the cemetery, close to 100 figures gathered at her grave site. There, in accordance with her wishes, Holiday was buried near her mother. Ralph Gleason later said in a fitting eulogy, "It is sad beyond words that she never knew how many loved her."

But love her they did, and the number of Holiday's admirers continued to rise in the ensuing years. Her more recent popularity is due in part to a filmed version of *Lady Sings the Blues*, which was released in 1972. The movie, starring singer Diana Ross, drew mixed reactions from Holiday's fans. Many of them praised Ross's performance but condemned the screenplay for being unfaithful to the facts of Holiday's life. Despite these protests, the movie was commercially successful and served to revive interest in Holiday. Her records were reissued, and an entirely new generation of listeners discovered her talent.

Artie Shaw, who worked with her in the 1930s, has pointed out that Holiday's style "has been copied and imitated by so many singers of popular music that the average listener of today cannot realize how original she actually was." Possessing a daring approach to phrasing and an uncanny sense of timing, she was an expert at delivering a song's meaning. "Lady made you feel—really feel—whatever she was singing," said jazz vocalist Joe Williams. By doing so, she extended the limits of popular music, making it meaningful by giving the songs incredible depth. "Nobody had the effect on people she had," claimed trumpeter Roy Eldridge.

Even when people who listen to Holiday's voice know nothing about her unhappy life, they still identify with the emotions—happy or sad—that her singing arouses. Her music persists because it is honest and direct. As singer and pianist Hazel Scott put it, "The thing I hope the kids don't miss—the ones who are just discovering Lady—is that she took a lot of the tragedy out of her life and made something beautiful out of it...She was always concerned about other people and very often she tried to bring to her music not sadness and despair but courage and love and the things you've got to have in order to cope...listen to her sing...and you'll know there were many dimensions to her."

*Holiday performing at the end of her career. "She was," according to jazz critic and longtime friend Leonard Feather, "sweet, sour, kind, mean, generous, profane, lovable, and impossible."*

# CHRONOLOGY

| | |
|---|---|
| 1915 | Born Eleanora Fagan in Baltimore, Maryland, on April 7 |
| 1927 | Moves to New York; settles in Harlem |
| 1930 | Sings professionally for the first time at Pod's and Jerry's in Harlem |
| 1933 | Cuts first record, "Your Mother's Son-in-Law" |
| 1935 | Plays the Apollo Theater; begins recording with Teddy Wilson; appears in the film *Symphony in Black* with Duke Ellington and His Orchestra |
| 1936 | Records "Billie's Blues," the first recording on which she receives solo billing |
| 1937 | Meets Lester Young; tours with the Count Basie Orchestra |
| 1938 | Tours with the Artie Shaw Orchestra |
| 1939 | Headlines at Café Society; records "Strange Fruit" |
| 1944 | Records "Lover Man" using an arrangement that features a string section |
| 1946 | Makes first solo appearance in a concert hall setting; appears in the film *New Orleans* |
| 1947 | Arrested for possession of narcotics; sentenced to a year and a day at the Federal Reformatory for Women at Alderson, West Virginia |
| 1948 | Released from prison; performs at Carnegie Hall; appears at the Strand Theater |
| 1949 | Arrested for possession of narcotics; tried and acquitted |
| 1952 | Begins recording for Norman Granz |
| 1954 | Makes first concert tour of Europe; performs at the first Newport Jazz Festival |
| 1956 | Arrested for possession of narcotics; *Lady Sings the Blues* is published |
| 1958 | Holiday records *Lady in Satin* with arranger Ray Ellis |
| 1959 | Dies on July 17 in New York City |

# FURTHER READING

Archer, Robyn, and Diana Simmonds. *A Star is Torn*. New York: Dutton, 1987.

Burnett, James. *Billie Holiday*. New York: Hippocrene Books, 1984.

Chilton, John. *Billie's Blues: The Billie Holiday Story, 1933–1959*. New York: Stein and Day, 1975.

Clayton, Buck. *Buck Clayton's Jazz World*. New York: Oxford University Press, 1987.

De Veaux, Alexis. *Don't Explain: A Song of Billie Holiday*. New York: Harper & Row, 1980.

Feather, Leonard. *From Satchmo to Miles*. New York: Stein and Day, 1971.

Gourse, Leslie. *Louis' Children: American Jazz Singers*. New York: Morrow, 1984.

Haskins, James. *Black Music in America: A History Through Its People*. New York: Crowell, 1987.

Holiday, Billie, with William Dufty. *Lady Sings the Blues*. New York: Penguin Books, 1984.

Maddocks, Melvin. *Billie Holiday*. Alexandria, VA: Time-Life, 1979.

Shaw, Arnold. *Black Popular Music in America: From the Spirituals, Minstrels, and Ragtime to Soul, Disco and Hip-hop*. New York: Schirmer Books, 1986.

_____.*52nd Street: The Street of Jazz*. New York: Da Capo, 1977.

White, John. *Billie Holiday: Her Life and Times*. New York: Universe, 1987.

# INDEX

# SELECTED DISCOGRAPHY

Billie Holiday's many moods have been captured on the following albums. Full of heartfelt vocals, these recordings are all currently available and should serve as a good introduction to her music.

*All or Nothing at All* (Verve)
*Billie's Blues* (Columbia)
*Body & Soul* (Verve)
*The Essential Billie Holiday* (Verve)
*The First Verve Sessions* (Verve)
*God Bless the Child* (Columbia)
*History of the Real Billie Holiday* (Verve)
*Billie Holiday: The Golden Years, vols. 1-2* (Columbia)
*Billie Holiday: Greatest Hits* (Columbia)
*Billie Holiday: Original Recordings* (Columbia)
*The Billie Holiday Songbook* (Verve)
*The Billie Holiday Story* (MCA)
*Billie Holiday Story, vols. 1-3* (Columbia)
*Jazz at the Philharmonic* (Verve)
*Lady Day* (Columbia)
*Lady in Satin* (Columbia)
*Lady Lives, vols. 1-3* (ESP)
*Lady Sings the Blues* (Verve)
*The Legend of Billie Holiday* (MCA)
*The Quintessential Billie Holiday, vols. 1-5* (Columbia)
*Sound of Jazz* (CSP)
*Stormy Blues* (Verve)

# PICTURE CREDITS

BUD KLIMENT lives in New York City and works for the Pulitzer Prize Board at Columbia University. He specializes in film and music writing and has contributed to the *Village Voice, Video,* and other periodicals. His writing has also appeared in *The Book of Rock Lists, The New Trouser Press Record Guide,* and *The Virgin Guide to New York*. He is the author of *Ella Fitzgerald,* part of the Chelsea House Black Americans of Achievement series, which was named one of the Best Books for the Teen Age by the New York Public Library.

# MELROSE SQUARE BLACK AMERICAN SERIES

*These highly acclaimed quality format paperback editions are profusely illustrated, meticulously researched and fully indexed. $3.95 ea.*

☐ **NAT TURNER:** Prophet and Slave Revolt Leader

☐ **PAUL ROBESON:** Athlete, Actor, Singer, Activist

☐ **ELLA FITZGERALD:** First Lady of American Song

☐ **MALCOLM X:** Militant Black Leader

☐ **JACKIE ROBINSON:** First Black in Professional Baseball

☐ **MATTHEW HENSON:** Arctic Explorer

☐ **SCOTT JOPLIN:** Composer

☐ **LOUIS ARMSTRONG:** Musician

☐ **SOJOURNER TRUTH:** Antislavery Activist

☐ **CHESTER HIMES:** Author and Civil Rights Pioneer

☐ **BILLIE HOLIDAY:** Singer

☐ **RICHARD WRIGHT:** Author

☐ **ALTHEA GIBSON:** Tennis Champion

☐ **JAMES BALDWIN:** Author

☐ **WILMA RUDOLPH:** Champion Athlete

☐ **SIDNEY POITIER:** Actor

☐ **JESSE OWENS:** Olympic Superstar

☐ **MARCUS GARVEY:** Black Nationalist Leader

☐ **JOE LOUIS:** Boxing Champion

☐ **HARRY BELAFONTE:** Singer & Actor

☐ **LENA HORNE:** Singer & Actor

The Saga of Five
Generations of

# A MISSISSIPPI FAMILY

By Barbara Johnson
With Mary Sikora

# RICHARD PRYOR

## THE MAN BEHIND THE LAUGHTER

**BIOGRAPHY**—The most famous comedian in America today—and the most controversial—Richard Pryor's life story reads like a work of exciting, if improbable fiction. His self-confessed beginnings in Peoria, Illinois, where his mother was a prostitute in his grandmother's bordello; his life on the streets as a young man; his sturggle to break into show business on his own uncompromising terms; his acknowledged use of cocaine and other drugs; and his near brush with death after a mystery fire at his home in California have all provided material for his shocking comic portrayals. If the past is an indicator of the future, Pryor will continue to shock, titillate and make the world laugh with him for many years to come.

# TO KILL A BLACK MAN

**By Louis E. Lomax**

A compelling dual biography of the two men who changed America's way of thinking—Malcolm X and Martin Luther King, Jr.

Louis E. Lomax was a close friend to both Malcolm X and Dr. Martin Luther King, Jr. In this dual biography, he includes much that Malcolm X did not tell in his auto-biography and dissects Malcolm's famous letters. Lomax writes with the sympathy and understanding of a friend but he is also quick to point out the shortcomings of both Dr. King and Malcolm X—and what he believed was the reasons for their failure to achieve their goals and to obtain the full support of all their people. And he does not hesitate in pointing a finger at those he believes to be responsible for the deaths of his friends. "A valuable addition to the available information on the murders of Martin Luther King, Jr. and Malcolm X," says the *Litterair Passport*. Louis Lomax gained national prominence with such books as *The Black Revolt*, *When The Word Is Given*, and *To Kill A Black Man*. At the time of his death in an automobile accident he was a professor at Hofstra University.

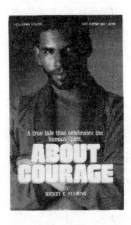

# TRIUMPH & TRAGEDY
## The True Story of the
# THE SUPREMES

By Marianne Ruuth

## No Holds Barred!

Marianne Ruuth interviewed former members of The Supremes, friends and associates for an in-depth look at those three young women that all of American fell in love with back in the 1960s. They were: Florence Ballard ("the shy one"), Mary Wilson ("the one many considered to be the most talented") and Diana Ross ("the one determined to become a star"), all from Detroit and all terribly innocent in the beginning. Florence became the figure of tragedy: She died very young, living on welfare. Mary, still performing, found something of a normal life for a star. . . and we all know that Diana realized her ambition of becoming a Superstar. Now read the real story behind the headlines and the gossip!

# JESSE JACKSON

By Eddie Stone

### An Intimate Portrait of the Most Charismatic Man in American Politics

He's dynamic, charming, intelligent and has more charisma than any man to rocket into the American political arena since John F. Kennedy. One of the country's most popular black leaders, he is not without his critics. To many he is just too flamboyant, others find his political ideas somewhat vague, still others call him a blatant opportunist. Nevertheless he has proven he can pull in the votes whether it's in Vermont, or Mississippi, or Michigan. Jackson will play a major—and far reaching—role in American politics in the years to come.